A Dumb American in a Strange Country: Finding God Where You Least Expect Him!

∽o∾

John Murphy

xulon
PRESS

Copyright © 2006 by John Murphy

*A Dumb American in a Strange Country:
Finding God Where You Least Expect Him!*
by John Murphy

Printed in the United States of America

ISBN 978-1-60034-411-4
ISBN 1-60034-411-9

All rights reserved solely by the author. The author guarantees all contents are original and do not infringe upon the legal rights of any other person or work. No part of this book may be reproduced in any form without the permission of the author. The views expressed in this book are not necessarily those of the publisher.

Unless otherwise indicated, Bible quotations are taken from the New International Version of the Bible, vii, copyright © 1978 by International Bible Society.

www.xulonpress.com

Dedication:

This book is dedicated to every reader who honestly decides to give God a fighting chance. I look forward to hearing your testimonies!

Contents

∽o∽

Part One: *The Internship!* 9

Chapter One: *Lunar Landing.* 11
Chapter Two: *This is Houston: Do you read?* 19
Chapter Three: *Houston, ah…we finally have contact!* 27
Chapter Four: *Going to the moon to find myself?* 37
Chapter Five: *Confused and VERY far from home.* 51
Chapter Six: *Refueling, Repairing, and Repenting.* 59

Part Two: *Strange Country? Dumb American?* 63

Chapter Seven: *My first real whiff.* 65
Chapter Eight: *First lasting impressions.* 73
Chapter Nine: *Only in Ukraine!* 81
Chapter Ten: *Learning to laugh…at yourself.* 87

Part Three: *Some God-lessons For the Road!* 93

Chapter Eleven: *Finding God's will isn't entirely doing God's will!* 95
Chapter Twelve: *God's plan and my personality.* 101

Chapter Thirteen: *Doubts, concerns, and answers.* *107*
Chapter Fourteen: *This just can't all be for nothing!* *113*
Chapter Fifteen: *Take it like a man and just believe!* *125*
Chapter Sixteen: *The only contingency plan that works*............*131*
Chapter Seventeen: *Once there was a missionary
                       who got saved…* *141*
Chapter Eighteen: *One happy ending and a few
                      happy beginnings*..*153*

Part One:
The Internship!

Chapter One
Lunar Landing

☙◦❧

March of 1993 is when it all began. "Well John," asked Kevin Larson, my seminary friend, "are you coming to Ukraine with us or not?"

"What? Who? Where? Ukraine?" I asked. "Why would I want to go to Ukraine? That's like, near Russia, isn't it? Isn't it, like, freezing cold over there all the time? After all, the only time I've ever been outside the United States was when I went to Canada on a summer fishing trip, which is understandable." At this point, Kevin's eye-rolling told both of us that we were in for a battle.

"But, Kevin," I barked, "I've never been on a mission trip before and that's probably because I'm happy where I am. Why would I want to leave America, even temporarily? Besides, I already know God's will for my life . . . after graduate school I'm heading back to my old stomping grounds, Long Island, and I'm bound to find a ministry because I grew up there. I mean, after all, it's God's will! Surely everything will fall into place. Right? So, Kevin, b u d d y, have a nice trip and we'll see you when you get back. Okay? Oh, and remember, my friend, I'll be praying for you!"

King David wrote, *"Delight yourself in the Lord and He will give you the desires of your heart" (Psalms 37:4).* Okay, well, what's that supposed to mean? Well, as a young seminary student, I thought it meant exactly what it said: "Follow the man upstairs and He'll give you WHATEVER YOU WANT! AMEN!" Pretty simple, isn't it? And in a sense that is true, but not exactly the way I interpreted it, as we'll soon see.

Teaching a confident young seminary student something about God's will is difficult, for obvious reasons. See, after high school I knew it all. After Bible College, though, I somehow knew a lot less. Then seminary taught me many things, but the most important thing it taught me was humility. I realized that even though I was receiving a Master's Degree, in the real world I was just graduating from nursery school. Seminary just reinforced Bible College's lessons: there is so much more out there to consider. "So sit back," I told myself, "and humbly enjoy the long ride to maturity." Someone aptly wrote, "Earning a Ph.D. simply introduces someone to all he doesn't know." Even though all I was getting was a MA, I could still relate.

Finally, once I got out into the real world I realized that I was just another dumb American in this big beautiful world. And somehow, someway, though I still can't explain it, God managed to get me onto that plane to Eastern Europe with Kevin's group of students, which is when the real fun started.

Speculating about how God succeeded still confounds me though. In Bible College, every freshman was required to take at least one class related to cross-cultural missions. However, I was the one student that was so positive I'd never become a missionary that I actually approached the missions professor, Linda Joyner, asking to be exempt. I told her, "Look, I'm sure the classes are great and all, but they're just not for me because there is just no possible way that I'll ever consider going to the mission field. Therefore, I really don't see how a missions-related class will help me. So why don't we just save ourselves a lot of time and frustration by allowing me to take a class that will actually be of some benefit to me? Am I making any sense?" Well, whether I made sense or not didn't matter; I still wound up taking the class against my will. I just waited until my senior year to do it. Apparently Professor Joyner had a knack for spotting stubborn horses a mile away, although her class didn't quite break this one. Kevin's invitation, on the other hand, was another story altogether.

What was I thinking? Leaving my comfort zone to go to the former Soviet Union? Was it temporary insanity? Was it just a weird dose of curiosity? Or was it God simply working out His perfect will for my life with or without my full consent? Although I'm sure there may have been a combination of factors, I'm also sure that God was very much involved. Our informal meeting with Beth Miller, who had already visited Ukraine, abruptly shattered any doubts about that one. Beth was also planning to accompany us this time around and Kevin and I were assuming that the meeting would purposely be encouraging and informative. All we got was the latter, though, which seemed a lot like a boot-camp-styled dose of reality. Beth assembled our little group and mainly tried to prepare us for the worst. "Well guys," she sighed, "how can I water this down for you? The mosquitoes are bigger than dinosaurs and there are no screens on the windows. So get ready for some long sleepless nights. Oh, and by the way, they love to bite you right between the toes. Sorry about that one! Anyway, what else should I tell you?" Kevin and I quickly exchanged glances while Beth proceeded with the gory details: "Oh, if you don't live in an apartment then you'll probably have an outhouse and instead of reading the newspaper there, you'll be wiping with it. And, in the dark, that can leave some serious scars if you're not careful. Take my word for it! Oh, and the food can also be a problem." Kevin's look of horror, as we left the meeting, was probably almost as scary as mine. "What the heck are we getting ourselves into?" we thought.

A few days later, Kevin, most likely attempting to pry the first smile out of me since our unforgettable Paris-Island-briefing, mustered up the courage to tell me something "positive" about all this. "Hey John," he poked, "ninety percent of those who go on their first mission trip decide to take another. And many actually wind up becoming full-time missionaries too. I just thought you should know that since I forgot to mention it earlier."

"Beautiful!" I chided with a frown. "Now you tell me!" Needless to say, that wasn't quite the kind of encouragement I was seeking because the mission field, especially the kind with T-Rex mosquitoes, was NOT FOR ME. PERIOD! But the tickets were already purchased and they were NON-REFUNDABLE. So it would only be a matter of time before we bit the bullet, boarded that Boeing 767, and . . . well, you'll see.

We flew over on KLM Dutch Airlines, and the pilot spoke in his native tongue, subsequently translating into English. Hearing Dutch for the first time really tickled me to the point of hysteria: "Unka aida eida faida . . . loud snorting sounds . . . unka bunka . . . Willy Wonka!" *(That's a paraphrase, in case you're wondering.)* Thanks to my nervous tension that hilarious pilot got me to laughing uncontrollably. In trying to get me to shut up, my team only encouraged me to laugh even louder until half of the plane was rolling in the aisles. And for the rest of the trip we were all giddy to the point of being obnoxious. I think the only reason the flight attendants didn't toss us out the hatch was because they also got a kick out of the whole scenario.

We finally touched down at Borispol International Airport, in Kiev, the capital city. I remember our group getting into a filthy old tractor-like vehicle and being shuttled to a large building that looked a lot like a cross between a medieval barn and a modern warehouse. It was dark, grimy, and older than Father Time. We must have stood in the center of that large vacant room for probably a good forty-five minutes, watching baggage-handlers drive by on their little yellow thingies.

Frustrated and exhausted, I asked, "Guys, when exactly are we going to the airport?"

"John," somebody remarked, "you're standing inside of it."

"No, seriously guys," I pressed, "when are we going to the airport?" The silent stares told me all I needed to know. I couldn't believe my eyes. This was Kiev's international terminal? Let's put it this way, it didn't take long for the culture shock to set in. In contrast to our hysterically fun-packed plane ride, cracking a smile at that moment was next to impossible. And, again, that looming question recurred, "What have we gotten ourselves into?"

From Kiev, our seventeen-hour bus trip to Crimea, that early June, seemed like one of the longest journeys I'd ever experienced in my 23 years on the planet, which is probably because it was. I felt like if we were to suddenly pass the Starship Enterprise that we should take that as a good sign meaning we were just about there. At 4 a.m., while periodically glancing out the window onto the Ukrainian landscape, I read several letters from my friends and relatives, all of them thousands of miles away. The reality was hitting me. But, believe it or not, that was the first and last time I would shed tears in Ukraine that summer.

When we finally arrived in Simferopol, our destination, David and I found out that we were the only ones chosen to live in a Crimean Tatar village called Dubke simply because we had taken one class on Islam in seminary. Obviously, preparedness wasn't exactly our strongest point in this particular operation.* Fortunately, being the two strapping young lads that we were, our priorities, rather than preaching, were twofold: 1) helping to build a house in the village for a needy family, and 2) digging a well that would provide water for the people.

Although David and I lacked some of the benefits that the other teams members might have had, like a toilet seat and running water, by the end of the summer our entire group envied us due to the wonderful host family we ended up with. We had lots of fun together, drank lots of tea, played lots of practical jokes, and ate lots of rice pilaf too. Their three-year old son, Timor, would not only drink coffee with us every morning, but he would also eat the leftover coffee grounds with a spoon when he was done. In fact, he not only ate the ones in his cup but also ate our leftovers too. So, you can just imagine that boredom was never an issue in that household. Attempting to communicate with our new friends was also quite the adventure. My Russian was so bad that I'd usually say, "You're welcome," when I meant, "thanks," but that doesn't even scratch the surface.

Since Dubke is a Tatar village on the outskirts of the city, only special buses or minivans will get you there. And because Dubke wasn't considered an official bus stop, one had to make a special request if the driver were to let you out there. Well, that's easier said than done when we're talking about a dumb American with almost no Russian under his belt. The first time I approached the bus driver, I said: "Astavatsa Dubka!" That supposedly meant: "Stop at

Dubke!" What I actually wound up saying, though, could be interpreted in at least two different ways: 1) "Stay in Dubke!" or 2) "Stay here you idiot!" The word "dub" in Russian literally means "log," but it's colloquially used to refer to a numbskull.

"What? I didn't understand you. Can you repeat it?" he requested.

"Astavatsa Dubka!" I demanded. At this point, even the beggars and roving alcoholics were cracking up.

"Ah, I still didn't quite catch that one! Get an interpreter, will you?" he prodded.

"Astavatsa Dubka!" I shouted, with a host of strange hand-gestures that the whole bus enjoyed watching. Incredibly, he stopped at Dubke, so I thought our little problem was finally solved. Hence, when I approached him the following day saying "Astavatsa Dubka!" I automatically assumed that the driver would completely understand me.

"I have no clue what you're saying!" he growled. "Get an interpreter, will you?"

"Astavatsa Dubka!" I pounced. It was clear that I was quickly becoming Mr. Popular because everyone wondered whether or not I was really calling the bus driver a "dub" *(idiot)*, including him.

"You're the idiot!" the driver jeered. "Sit down and shut up already!" Miraculously, however, we did manage to stop at Dubke. Although the driver probably wanted to strangle me, the people on the bus couldn't get enough of me and they anxiously looked forward to whatever day three would bring.

Actually, day three was a lot easier because we finally made a clear connection. "Astavatsa Dubka!" I appealed.

"Yeah, I know!" he screamed, shoeing me away with his hand. "I know already!" Nevertheless, the realization that everything would be a chore in this strange new place really hit me hard that week. Regardless of how helpless I felt on that bus, though, in my mind I was still in the driver's seat because it wouldn't be long before I'd be back in my own car in my own country, speaking my own lingo. "All of this chaos in my life is just temporary," I thought.

Originally, my purpose for the trip to Ukraine was simply to prepare myself for ministry in America. I figured I'd learn some lessons about maturity that I probably wouldn't be able to pick up at home or in a book, further equipping me for ministering in the New York area. "Alright," was my attitude, "let's go over for a couple of months and suffer a while, save a few souls, show the natives how it's done, show God how good a person you're becoming, possibly even grow up a little in the process, and then God will surely bless your ministry in New York." Essentially, this trip was sort of a supplement to whatever I was getting in the classroom. Unbeknownst to me, the "chaos" on that Ukrainian bus didn't even begin to compare with the chaos in my own spiritual life.

The fact is that my favorite bus driver taught me something I never would have learned in seminary. That experience caused me to feel utterly helpless; it made me feel totally dependent on God in manners I'd never felt before. It helped me to grow by turning my book knowledge into reality. It's like what Mother Theresa said: "Nobody can say, 'Jesus is all I need,' until Jesus is all you've got." Until you've really been there, you haven't really been there. And if you haven't really been there, then you don't fully understand no matter how much book knowledge you may have. Seminary taught me what the Bible says about needing to depend on God. That little bus ride, by contrast, forced me to literally depend on Him fully, finally helping me to truly understand what that actually means. In retrospect, I can't help but say: *"Wow, what a feeling!"* Why? Because when we're in complete control, God is not, meaning that He's then forced to share center stage with us. You see, until we're totally relying on Him one hundred percent, in the truest sense of the word, we'll seldom clearly hear His voice. We'll rarely grasp, entirely, what He's trying to say to us personally. That's why cross-cultural mission trips are so crucial to one's spiritual health. In the ultimate battle for our hearts, mission trips are one of just a few tools that succeed in giving God a fighting chance. They're famous for changing lives because they stretch Christians enough to put them in God's back yard, allowing Him to speak more clearly to them than ever before. I'm living proof of that and in a little while I'll explain why.

Paul wrote in 1 Corinthians 8:1-3, *"Knowledge puffs up, but love builds up. The man who thinks he knows something does not yet know as he ought to know. But the man who loves God is known by God."* Pride, like all sins, usually delivers the opposite of what it promises. Instead of exhibiting our strengths, as intended, it manifests our weaknesses. After mine became crystal clear to me, I discovered that what I really needed far exceeded a mere lesson in maturity. I also needed to learn what loving God was all about in a way that would radically change my perception of His will for my life. Psalms 37:4 had always been a verse I could quote effortlessly: *"Delight yourself in the Lord and he will give you the desires of your heart."* The problem was that I only had a seminary view of what that really meant. God, however, was about to change that forever.

The Crimean Tatars are a Muslim people group who were deported by Stalin to some of the Soviet block countries near Afghanistan, such as Uzbekistan, Turkmenistan, and Tajikistan, and they were afforded the opportunity to return to Crimea after the fall of the USSR.

Chapter Two
This is Houston: Do you read?

☙○❧

In November of 2002, I spoke at a church in Virginia for their area-wide Thanksgiving service. A teenager from an adjacent town, who was considering becoming a Christian, happened to have been present that evening. Just weeks earlier he had begun attending one of the other local churches and was apparently dealing with some serious issues in his life. I opened my sermon that evening with the following statement, "Someone once said – 'The worst thing in the life of an atheist is when he's extremely grateful for something and has nobody to thank'." Although there's certainly truth to that statement, I never thought it would actually impact someone's life. I more-or-less just used it as an icebreaker that evening. Well, incredibly, that boy gave his life to Christ the following week, later informing me that it was that particular thought that deeply affected him due to the inner sense of emptiness with which he had been struggling. Having nobody to thank for all of the blessings in his life was something he understood well and that's what made the difference. Amazing! That's just another vivid reminder that some lessons are self-learned, some are taught by others, and then there are those that only God Himself can teach us. As for me, discovering the true meaning of Psalms 37:4 happened to be one of those unique God-lessons. And it was one lesson I'd never forget.

The summer of 1993 was chock-full of unexpected spiritual mountaintop experiences but two of them especially etched themselves into my memory bank. Both occurred in two Muslim villages named Pionerskaya and Dubke. Pionerskaya was a village that Kevin and several others had been surveying. They'd visit each house, asking whether or not the people had any specific needs, in hopes of establishing quality contacts for missionaries already laboring in that region. Kevin even relayed a story about how, on one particular day, while their group's translator was off somewhere with the rest of the crew, a Tatar man from that village approached him and asked, "Shprecken ze Duetch?"

"No . . . ah, nein!" Kevin replied.

"Ah, Angliski . . . English, huh?" the man inquired.

"Yes . . . ah, da!" Kevin answered.

"English, hmm?" responded the man. "One, two, three, four, five . . . yes . . . no . . . thank you very much . . . To be or not to be? . . . not to be!" And with that, realizing that he had already exhausted the limits of his English vocabulary, the Tatar man just smiled and went about his business. You never knew what to expect in strange new places, which is what I learned when I took a break from mixing cement and joined Kevin's group for a day.

We visited one woman who just couldn't believe that we had come all the way from America to ask her if she needed anything. "It's hard to find neighbors or even family members who ask those kinds of questions," she noted, "let alone perfect strangers from another country." "Moreover," she added, "I'm a Muslim woman and you're all Christians. How could you care about someone like me?" she wondered.

"We love you very much," I affirmed, "because Jesus Christ loves you very much. He always has and He always will." I'll never forget how the tears streamed down her face at that very moment. Though she regained her composure somewhat, the tears continued for another forty-five minutes. She had never held a Bible in her hands but still refused when we offered to give her one.

It was clear, however, that her refusal was solely based on fear. "What would my husband say if he found out that I accepted a Bible?" she asked. Leaving that house was difficult because God had been in that kitchen with all of us. Even though the entire episode was laden with a supernatural feeling throughout, we still sorrowfully chocked it up as another missed opportunity. Oftentimes, though, the first person God is looking to convert on a mission trip is the one taking the mission trip instead of the national, which was something I still hadn't realized at that point. My big game plan was to change the world, but God's big game was changing my world first. And God wasn't entirely finished here just yet.

We got about a half mile from her house, walking down the old dirt road overlooking the village, when I suddenly sensed an undeniable urge to turn back and leave that Bible with her. I wasn't about to give up that easy. When I turned around, in the distance I saw our new friend running toward us as fast as she could. "I was just wondering," she huffed, while catching her breath, "if that Bible offer was still available." And although I never saw her again, I know for sure that something special happened that day, even in my life.

Dubke staged the second event. Although our main projects there consisted of physical labor, we also decided to conduct one Vacation Bible School program before our departure. Hosting a VBS in a Muslim village, adjacent to a field where a mosque was being built, definitely had "potential for disaster" written all over it! We, nevertheless, decided to trust God and hope for the best, which usually works pretty effectively. One reason why we were confident enough to attempt this was because Chuck Philips, an American missionary working with Tatars in Dubke, had been tilling the soil with God's mighty rotor tiller for at least a year or more. And everything went without a hitch, except for one little bump in the road called: "Our Closing Program." In addition to our group of about 100 kids, many parents also came, as was expected. Unfortunately, some uninvited guests from the local mosque decided to crash the party.

The local mullah *(Muslim preacher)*, along with a group of his henchmen, raised their voices in unison: "Get out of our village immediately!" The mullah proceeded to take issue by claiming that we were invading his spiritual jurisdiction with our propaganda, all without the required authorization. "Who do you think you are?" he shouted. "Who gave you the right to preach from the Bible here? Dubke is our spiritual territory and these people are my spiritual children! And this is our final warning! So I think it's time for you to go."

Not only were we intimidated but we were also concerned about the future of the work there. On top of that, there were some questions we had to ask ourselves: "Is Satan posing this threat or are we to blame for this mess? Did we fast and pray before planning this VBS? Were we trying to do too much too soon? Were we too impatient to wait for God's timing? Were we selfishly or foolishly rushing God into something too risky too soon? Were we so focused on our imminent departure date that we actually lost sight of God's will?" Besides having the wrong tooth extracted by a delirious dentist when I was six years old, and aside from my brief encounter with a Tatar doctor and a scalpel *(I'll cover that later)*, this had to be one of the longest hours of my life. Mentally, spiritually, psychologically, and even physically speaking, we certainly had a lot to chew on during that standoff.

"Well," you ask, "what happened next?" At this point, a much larger crowd had gathered because of the commotion, increasing the nervous tension in the air. A few from our group had formed a prayer circle off to the side, but I didn't join them because I wasn't about to miss this for anything. Sure, I was praying, alright, but I was right in the middle of the circle with my eyes and ears wide open just in case God decided to show up. This was like Elijah versus the prophets of Baal; like David against Goliath; like King Kong versus Godzilla; like the Terminator versus . . . you know . . . that other Terminator. Well, you get the idea.

Chuck smiled and spoke calmly, "In the Qur'an, chapter 10:94, it says that anyone who has questions regarding the truth should consult 'the People of the Book,' who are clearly understood to be Christians and Jews."

"Yes, I'm well aware of that verse," retorted the mullah, "but the Holy Qur'an also instructs Muslims not to associate themselves with Jews and Christians."

"Fascinating!" Chuck replied. "I don't think I've ever read that verse before. Could you show it to me in your Qur'an?"

All you could hear in that field was a gentle breeze and the turning of pages as the mullah searched . . . and searched some more . . . and continued his meaningless search. Finally, he closed his Qur'an and said, "Well, I can't find it right now but I know it's in there somewhere. In any case, that's not the point here. What is the point is that you have no right to be here without our permission, which should be the end of this meaningless discussion. So, I'll tell you one last time, 'Get out of my village'." Ouch! That wasn't exactly the response we were hoping for but, of course, he had something we apparently lacked: LEVERAGE. What we did have, however, proved to be much greater in the final analysis.

Just then, a voice rang out of the crowd. It was a young Muslim mother, whose child had been attending the VBS. "I have something to say!" she announced. "I really can't say that I've known any of these Americans very long. I'll even admit that completely trusting them or agreeing with much of what they say is something I'm not yet ready to do. But I can tell you that they're spending quality time with our children and they're also teaching them some good moral principles. In fact, one of them seems to be a type of love we've never really experienced before; they call it 'the love of Jesus.' In fact, they're even showing that love by building a house for a needy woman and her family here. They're also digging a well for our whole village, and they're hugging our children too, which is something we often fail to do ourselves." Then, in turning to face the mullah, she said, "As for you, I'm a little shocked that you consider yourself to be our spiritual leader. Personally, I haven't seen your face in two years. So, if my opinion counts for anything here, I'd say that if anybody should leave today then it should be you!" After a short bit of silence came a thundering applause from the crowd that not only sent shivers down my spine but also left an indelibly permanent impression on my life, as the mullah and company made their way to the exit.

"Open the eyes of my heart Lord . . . I want to see you," are the familiar words of a popular worship song these days. Paul reflects this sentiment in Ephesians 1:17-18: *"I keep asking that the God of our Lord Jesus Christ, the glorious Father, may give you the Spirit of wisdom and revelation, so that you may know Him better. I pray also that the eyes of your heart may be enlightened in order that you may know the hope to which He has called you, the riches of His glorious inheritance in the saints."* Ultimately, that's where God's will begins for all of us. We need to be able to see God in our everyday lives with the eyes of our hearts, not just our minds, and only then will we see His will clearly. Oftentimes, however, Christians need to undergo a serious operation for that to occur, whether they realize it or not. During a sermon, Ross Brodfuehrer, a minister at Southeast Christian Church in Louisville, Kentucky, recalled the Pharisees who criticized the blind man whose sight had been restored in John 9, and then he remarked, "Frequently, a man's cataracts are in his mind instead of his eyes." Consequently, many Christians never accomplish God's will for their lives because of their spiritual cataracts. By contrast, others eventually do but only because they're willing to get onto God's operating table, which is exactly where I was after those two life-changing experiences that summer. The Great Physician also tends to be a great optician and He can definitely open our eyes to a lot of things when we place the scalpel in His hand, for a change.

Several years back, an American missionary named Georges Carillet spoke to a group of Ukrainian Christians about Proverbs 29:18, which reads, *"Where there is no vision, the people perish."* Georges described how one's culture typically affects one's view of the Scriptures, which can be awfully misleading at times. Georges described that in the States, for example, strategic planning is so highly esteemed that it's considered paramount to practically everyone's success regardless of their occupation. Even many spiritual establishments have come to believe that goal setting based on a specific consensus-met mission statement, reflecting their unique "vision," is the first order of business. Hence, a "vision" is the modern American equivalent to the ultimate dream destination or most desirable end product for any organization or individual. Sadly, due to the American corporate world's influence on the Church, even prayer usually takes a back seat to designing clear objectives for the purpose of fulfilling the sacred "vision." Thus, many American

Christians cite Proverbs 29:18 as proof of the need for strategic planning. Although that may suit them just fine, it's not at all what Solomon was talking about. Solomon used the word "vision" here to literally mean divine revelation through a prophet or seer, which is always directly from the Lord, unlike many fallible consensus-based visions out there. Immediately, Georges reached for his glasses in order to read a Bible verse but realized that he left them in his office. So, just before he went to retrieve them, I quipped, "Hey Georges, without vision the people perish."

"Not funny!" was his comeback. Two weeks later, a guest speaker from the US quoted that verse at our church in Crimea, using it in that same flawed context. That wasn't funny either because spiritual cataracts can affect us all.

Dr. Jack Cooper is an ophthalmologist in California who has performed some pretty impressive cataract surgeries, enabling many people to regain their sight. He also has a chart on his office wall that reads: *"For God so loved the world that He gave His one and only Son, that whoever believes in him shall not perish but have eternal life" (John 3:16)*. When people get their bandages off and discover that they can see again they're obviously thrilled beyond measure. Once they see the chart, he then takes the opportunity to tell them about "the Light of the World," Jesus Christ, and the spiritual sight that only He can offer.

Fanny Crosby was a great Christian hymn writer who was blind from birth and she'd always claim to have been thankful for that. "Because the first thing I'll ever see," she'd say, "is the face of Jesus Christ." How's your vision holding up these days? If it's a bit blurred then don't worry because there is hope. For now, just keep reading.

Chapter Three
Houston, ah . . .
we finally have contact!

∽o∾

"Wait a minute!" you may be thinking. "Are you telling me that those two particular events, that summer, literally changed your entire life? How? I mean, sure, they were somewhat unique, but they weren't, like, out of the body experiences or anything. Please tell me what the big deal is already!" Well, I'll get to that a bit later in the program. For now, let me just do a little preaching first. Throughout the Bible we see that many of God's servants suffered in a variety of ways, but very few, if any, suffered from boredom. Especially in the Old Testament, doing or witnessing spectacular things was commonplace for the great men and women of God. Their lives were basically inundated with magnificent events. Notice, though, that the Scriptures frequently talk about God being "with" His servants, which is significant here. Though all Christians may have the benefit of God's forgiveness, that doesn't necessarily mean that they all have the benefit of His imminently active presence within their lives. Just because God may have forgiven us, and even may dwell inside of us, that certainly doesn't always mean that He's doing supernatural things in and through our lives. There's a

BIG difference between God being "in" us and Him being "with" us.

The author of 2 Chronicles, in verse two of chapter fifteen, writes, *"The Lord is with you when you are with Him."* Paul even explains how God's indwelling presence can be wholly dormant within a Christian's life due to habitual sin *(Ephesians 4:30)*. That's when Christianity turns into boring religion. In fact, verse eighteen, though referring to the Gentiles, still provides insight for us here. Paul exhorts the Ephesians not to continue acting like Gentiles due to the potential consequences: *"They are darkened in their understanding and separated from the life of God... due to the hardening of their hearts."*

Several key points stand out here but let's chat before discussing this passage. You may posit that Paul's words in this section don't relate to you but remember that sin comes in all packages. For a minute, let's stop thinking about serial killers, drug addicts, temple prostitutes, and bank robbers. Let's think about ourselves instead. Most folks, especially those of us who grew up in the Church, haven't done those things. On the other hand, there may be some of us who inadvertently value our computers, TV's, stocks, video games, shopping time, or golf outings, more than we do our quiet time with the Lord, or the time we're supposed to set aside for our families. Right? Maybe we've also developed attitudes, or even lifestyles, that have categorically restricted God or even shut Him out altogether. My previous attitude about missions: case in point! Most of us tend to gloss over our weak points; that's why they're our weak points. But that one tiny facet of our lives that we often tend to ignore, sometimes acting as though it's totally insignificant, is frequently *the most important aspect in God's eyes*. And until we root out that stronghold, we'll still be *living in sin*.

Having said that, let's note the relevance of Paul's words in Ephesians 4:18. First, sin both separates us from God as well as from *"the life of God,"* which surely refers to His providential activity and blessings in our lives. In other words, don't expect God to perform miracles in your life if you're keeping Him at a safe distance. If you want God to enter your life in an extraordinary way then you've got to step out of your comfort zone and attempt to do some extraordinary things for Him first. If you want God to show up, then first give Him a good reason to. That's why James wrote, *"The prayer of a righteous man is powerful and effective" (5:16)*. The point is that if you let God get a little closer to your heart then you're bound to be surprised by the wonders He will perform in your life. The center of God's will is where God is, which, by the way, is exactly where He happens to be waiting for us. So don't expect Him to be 'with' you until you decide to meet Him there.

Second, Paul highlights the essential futility and emptiness found in that separation from God in the following verse, *"Having lost all sensitivity, they have given themselves over to sensuality... with a continual lust for more" (Ephesians 4:19)*. Try to read this verse and apply it your own situation. Again, let's not think about the Temple of Artemis here. Rather, let's think about the issues keeping God at bay in our own lives. Are you there yet? Good. Here, Paul adds that this type of lifestyle ends in corruption "by its deceitful desires."

Third, turning off God's power and influence in our lives, through sin, simultaneously flips the on-switch for Satan's workshop. And that's when boring religion turns cuckoo! *"Do not give the devil a foothold,"* is Paul's advice in verse 27.

Someone once noted that the word "closer" sums up the whole pattern of human history. In the beginning, the Garden of Eden unmistakably manifested God's intimate relationship with man before sin altered it. Gladly, though, Scripture demonstrates that God has been on a perpetual quest for reunion with him ever since. After the Exodus, God's presence resided in the Tabernacle. Later, the Lord had Solomon build the temple where He would dwell, though access to His presence was very limited at best. In chapter one of John's Gospel, the apostle records one of God's giant steps in our direction: *"The Word became flesh and lived for a while among us. We have seen His glory, the glory of the one and only Son, who came from the Father, full of grace and truth" (v. 14)*. Though the incarnation was one step, the cross was yet another, and because of Christ's sacrifice we were given God's own indwelling presence to live inside of us. Now that's **close**, but it's still not quite the end of the story. The apostle John brings us even closer to God, in the book of Revelation, as we worship before His very throne in heaven.

Abraham was pretty special because in addition to having God's email address and cell phone number, he also had them memorized. Abraham was almost always in God's vicinity. In fact, he's uniquely referred to as God's *"friend"* several times in Scripture *(2 Chronicles 20:7; Isaiah 41:8; James 2:23)* because of his remarkable dedication to fulfilling God's will regardless of the cost. Concerning Abraham's most famous assignment, Henry and Richard Blackaby wrote, "In response to Abraham's obedience, God spared Isaac's life . . . Abraham . . . learned that when people are willing to give everything they have to God, God will supply all they need . . . Most spiritual leaders . . . make commitments; few offer absolute submission. God continues to look for those who are radically yielded to Him in every part of life so He may reveal His power to a watching world" *(Blackaby, pp. 52, 103-04)*. One obvious result of that friendship was the birth of Christ Himself, through the line of Abraham's son Isaac.

First Samuel records another tremendous example of sacrificial obedience. In the first two chapters we see the ancient version of Wonder Woman. Her name is Hannah. Despite the ridicule she faced daily, a result of her barrenness, often bringing her to the point of tears, she never once blamed God for her plight. Instead, she continued to rely on God through fervent prayer and a spotless heart. In fact, her motives were so pure that she even promised God that, in the event that He decided to grant her a son, she would in-turn give him back to the Lord to be raised in the temple for the priesthood. Now that's the kind of attitude that God is looking for! That's that miracle-working, spine-tingling, here-I-am-Lord-let's-conquer-the-universe-together kind of faith! After she made good on that promise, God not only salvaged the priesthood through her son Samuel, but He also gave her three other sons and two daughters to boot.

Miracles and blessings are always available to us but only when we make ourselves available to Him on His terms. Jesus said, *"You are my friends if you do what I command" (John 15:14)*. It's that same close relationship with God that's precisely what all of us need in order to experience God's sovereign activity in our everyday lives. Now, while those two events that summer may not have been considered miraculous per se, denying that God's presence encircled us would be nothing short of lunacy. The truth is that if God used Hannah and Abraham to save both the priesthood and the entire world, respectively, then just imagine what He can do through *"friends"* like you and me.

Unfortunately, many of us often forget that what Jesus usually commands requires immense sacrifice. Someone correctly noted that Christianity will never bring true fulfillment into our lives unless Jesus Christ has first place in our hearts. Until we've literally experienced that for ourselves we'll never genuinely comprehend how true that really is. As a result, many foolishly opt for a more comfortable version of "Christianity" by categorizing any serious expressions of faith as mere "fanaticism." They may say, "JESUS? YES! THE BIBLE? NO!" Or they may pull the Felix-Syndrome by only seeking God when it's convenient for them *(Acts 24:25)*. Or they may point to verses like Psalm 34:8, *"Taste and see that the Lord is good."* "A tiny spoon-full of faith every once in a while," they reason, "can even be a healthy thing." But they forget that when Peter alluded to that Psalm, in 1 Peter 2:3, he was writing to Christians who were willingly sacrificing their lives for their faith, under the persecutions of the Roman Emperor Nero. Because they had authentically savored the satisfaction people receive by giving Jesus their hearts, they were unwilling to relinquish that even in the face of death. In fact, according to tradition, Peter was forced to watch his wife's crucifixion just before his own, and during her suffering, he allegedly repeated a single phrase to her, "Remember the Lord; remember the Lord." Then Peter, himself, took his turn at facing the cross.

Believe it or not, all of this relates to the impact of those two significant events on my life during that summer. How? Well, it was then that I honestly discovered, for the first time in my life, the colossal distinction between receiving God's forgiveness, as God's child, and standing in the center of God's will, as His friend. Through those two experiences, combined with other circumstances on that brief internship, God finally succeeded in opening the eyes of my heart. He finally convinced me that the greatest place to live on this earth is smack-dab in the middle of His will, regardless of its circumstances or location on a map. And it didn't take a miracle for that to happen, which, if you ask me, is pretty miraculous.

"Okay, that's nice," you say, "but how did that help you see the real meaning of Psalm 37:4?" Well, we're slowly getting to that one too. Charles Colson is a famous Christian author who went from the White House to a prison cell in the early seventies for his involvement in the famous Watergate Scandal. He was not only one of Nixon's key advisors but also a fellow cohort in the conspiracy. It was in the state penitentiary where Jesus finally got his undivided attention for the first time. Consequently, Prison Fellowship Ministries was formed to spread the good news of Christ throughout the world's prisons. Several years after his release, he was interviewed by a renowned disc jockey in Australia who asked him to sum up the meaning of the two divergent lives he had been afforded to live. Noticing that in just twenty seconds they'd be off the air, he promptly answered, "If my life stands for anything, it is the truth of the teaching of Jesus Christ: *'Whoever wants to save his life will lose it, but whoever loses his life for me will find it. What good will it be for a man if he gains the whole world, yet forfeits his soul?'" (Matthew 16:25-26).* With that, despite the perplexed look of the host, the program concluded. In the introduction of his book *Who Speaks for God?* Colson explains, "I had spent my first forty years seeking the whole world, to the neglect of my soul, but what I couldn't find in my quest for power and success – that is, true security and meaning – I discovered in prison where all the worldly props had been stripped away, and by God's grace, I lost my life in order that I might find true life in Christ."

Charles Colson quickly became one of my favorite authors after the summer of 1993 because we had something in common. It wasn't because I had a criminal record or because I had ever rubbed shoulders with the president; it was because God taught us the same exact lesson. You see, even though I was a seminary student preparing for the ministry, I was so spiritually near-sighted that I might as well have been an incarcerated pariah. God's will was fine and dandy as long as it didn't get in the way of my own. It reminds me of the attitude of one Catholic girl in Yonkers, New York, during the Pope's visit several years ago. "Oh, we just love the Pope," she told the reporter. "Sure, he preaches against abortion and premarital sex, but he also says that even if we do those kinds of things that God still loves us and will forgive us anyway. So, hey, that works for me!"

In my case, I even had a list of so-called "reasons" why God was calling me back to New York. "You know," I'd say, "only former New Yorkers can effectively minister in New York. Since I grew up there, they'll surely welcome me back with open arms." Not only did that limit God by assuming that He couldn't build his Church there through non-native New Yorkers, but it was also blatantly false. After all, although my father was raised in Virginia, he still had two very productive ministries in New York. Lying to others is one thing; lying to yourself is quite another. Yet, I was indeed guilty of both. I was becoming a missionary to myself with God as my chief sponsor and "I love New York!" as my main impetus. I was like Khrushchev who, in response to the critics claiming that he believed in God because of his frequent usage of phrases like "God willing," or "for God's sake," proclaimed, "I am a staunch atheist and God knows it!" Like the former Soviet leader, having it both ways was the only way I'd have it. So that summer of 1993 changed a great deal. However, I still lived the first twenty-three years of my life thinking that God's will couldn't really be God's will if it didn't coincide with John's will. In other words, God still had His work cut out for Him.

David Ferguson writes about a couple he counseled because of their little boy's anger spurts. Once, while visiting with the family, Ferguson noticed one significant cause of the problem. In reality, their son was starving for attention, not because Daddy never spent any time with little Johnny but simply because Daddy never spent any quality time with him. It was frustrating playing with Daddy because he always played Daddy's game Daddy's way. While Johnny often begged Daddy to get down on the floor and help him with his blocks, Daddy preferred relaxing in his recliner while tossing velcro darts at the dartboard they originally bought for their son. Johnny's job was going back and forth to fetch and retrieve the darts for dear old Dad. Sure, Johnny got lots of attention but it was the kind that did more harm than good, for it showed the little boy that he was more of a household chore than the object of his father's love and affection. Of course anger was just the natural reaction of a child who felt more like a responsibility than a son *(Ferguson, pp. 66-67)*. The sad truth is that God and little Johnny could easily develop a modern day support group because you and I are often a lot like Daddy in our dealings with the Almighty. And, like Daddy, we usually suffer greatly because of it too.

I vividly recall a stirring article my Dad wrote in which he cited from "The Atlantan," a periodical published in an American federal prison. The article centered on the Christmas season and endeavored to analyze the concept of "imprisonment" while deciding whether or not it was limited solely to the people behind bars. "Christmas in prison," the article read, "is a time of reminiscence, of nostalgia, and of sadness. It's a time when a man seeks company, activity, and noise, to prevent himself from entering that part of his mind wherein he might feel embarrassed should he betray his thoughts. The prison takes on an air of hysteria. Even late in the night when the lights have gone out, the men stand at the bars and shout, beating metal on metal. Are they celebrating? No. They are defeating thought. They are driving back fear of themselves. Finally, the shouting will die down. Men will lie awake in the early morning thinking of their past Christmases surrounded by laughing children. Vows are sworn that future Christmases will be spent as Christmas should be; at home with family and friends, surrounded by kindness and love. Some will remember those vows and keep them. Others will remember them only when they have returned for more walled Christmases. Some will never have a chance to put their vows to the test." To conclude, my father propounded the need for a little introspection by posing this inquiry, "Could it be that all the business of the season, the commercialism, the festiveness, the celebrating, and the drunkenness, are but the sound and fury of men running from reality; running from themselves?"

The article really spoke to me because it accentuated my own "imprisonment." I hadn't been locked up somewhere but I had been a prisoner to my own selfish will, which caused me to inadvertently flee from both God and from myself. My spiritual vision was so warped that I couldn't even see it happening. In actuality, there were greater and more satisfying desires deep within myself, but my sinful attitude blinded me to the possibilities. How tragic! I was like that New York resident back in the early eighties, who desperately needed to get somewhere fast. Instead, he ended up in the local newspaper, never actually arriving at his destination. Upon entering his car on Long Island, he discovered that it would only go in reverse. Fully remiss and willingly disregarding everyone's safety, including his own, he insanely did the unthinkable by hopping onto the Long Island Expressway. What's even more staggering is that he wasn't stopped until he reached the Staten Island toll booth, which would have normally been at least a forty-five minute ride with the car in drive. Likewise, I had been heading in my own direction on my own terms, discounting everyone else's feelings but my own. Thankfully, God, on His perfect terms and according to His perfect timetable, caught up to me.

Chapter Four
Going to the moon to find myself?

※

In the mid-nineties, I was visiting with my oldest sister in New York. After about a week with Joy's family, my irritation with her youngest daughter, Alyssa, had reached its saturation point. I tried to be patient with Alyssa all week, refusing to correct her whenever I sensed even the slightest bit of selfishness, but I had finally reached my limit. After a kids' pool party, we were all headed back home in the car. At the party, Alyssa had received some new paint supplies and all I wanted to do was take a quick peek at them. When I politely made my request, however, it appeared that she too had had enough of old Uncle John. So she snatched her paints, screaming, "No! Don't touch them! They're mine!" Well, I felt it was high time to set the record straight by commenting on how selfish Alyssa was acting, but my sister's comeback shut me up in a hurry: "John, you're twenty-five; she's three. Give her back her paints!" Admittedly, she had a point. Sometimes, all we really need is a little perspective in order to see the bigger picture, which God liberally offers to hearts that are receptive. James, even regarding the fazing of life's disappointments, writes: *"If any of you lacks wisdom, he should ask God, who gives generously to all without finding fault, and it will be given to him" (James 1:5).* Although we may never get answers to all of the why-questions in life, at least God promises to provide open hearts with the strength and wisdom necessary for surviving whatever ordeal it is we're facing. What a promise indeed!

In the big scheme, if I may take the liberty of comparing myself with Charles Colson again, there's very little difference between preaching to a congregation each week and abusing one's political power if both are running from God. In a sense, I was like Pharaoh during the eighth and ninth plagues in Exodus 10. Amidst the eighth plague, he initially agreed to only release the men, but subsequently made concessions regarding the women and children during the ninth. Yet, he still followed that up with a quid pro quo: *"only leave your flocks and herds behind" (Exodus 10:24)*. The fact is that whenever we practice partial obedience we're living completely outside the will of God. And whenever we step outside of His will, even just a little bit, putting God on a leash becomes second nature to us. Once God is restricted from an area in our lives, it's only a matter of time before He's banned from others too. And before we know it, God's will turns invisible because it's of no interest to us anymore. The only thing that really matters then is what we want. That's when "So, hey, that works for me!" becomes our attitude regardless of how absurd the excuse may be. Let's not forget, that aside from the vacuum that partial obedience forms in our lives, our spiritual insurance policies might be a bit too flimsy to handle some of the other adverse outcomes that conceivably ensue. Just ask Azariah, Judah's former king. He was one of the few who did what was right in the eyes of the Lord, yet he was still stricken with leprosy because he didn't stop idolatry in the land *(2 Kings 15:3-5)*.

Solomon, speaking about true wisdom writes, *"The path of the righteous is like the first gleam of dawn, shining ever brighter till the full light of day. But the way of the wicked is like deep darkness; they do not know what makes them stumble . . . Above all else, guard your heart, for it is the wellspring of life" (Proverbs 4:18-19, 23)*. Notice how the heart is the heart of the matter. As with our physical bodies, when our hearts deteriorate everything else follows suit. It's when our selfish hearts are vulnerably unkempt that spiritual cataracts develop to the point that we start failing to even notice that we're heading in the wrong direction. By contrast, when we guard our hearts and choose undiluted righteousness instead of our own comfy version of God's will for our lives, which is the mistake I had been making, then our vision dramatically improves. We finally begin seeing past our noses and things that never made sense to us before start coming together. Even our lives start making sense because we're finally being honest enough to let God show us who we really are inside. That's one reason why Jesus taught that loving God with ALL of our hearts is the greatest commandment of all *(Matthew 22:37)*.

Deuteronomy is my favorite book in the Torah because, like Malachi, it's one big-hairy-audacious reminder of how important heart-felt, heart-driven, heart-filled, worship, service, and obedience, literally are. I also love the Psalms for that very same reason. Besides, David is even alluded to as *a man after his [God's] own heart (1 Samuel 13:14)*, possibly because of his pure heart for worship *(2 Samuel 23:1)*, his tremendous example to others *(2 Samuel 3:36)*, his unselfishness *(1 Samuel 30:21-31)*, his love for even his enemies *(1 Samuel 24:4-7; 2 Samuel 1:24)*, his humble perspective *(2 Samuel 16:10-14)*, his passion for justice *(2 Samuel 4:11-12)*, or his inspiring compassion *(2 Samuel 9)*, among the many other godly traits he exhibited.

At the end of his reign, David said, *"And you, my son Solomon, acknowledge the God of your father, and serve Him with wholehearted devotion and with a willing mind, for the Lord searches every heart and understands every motive behind the thoughts. If you seek Him, He will be found by you; but if you forsake Him, He will reject you forever" (1 Chronicles 28:9)*. The following chapter goes on to record David's prayer: *"I know, my God, that you test the heart and are pleased with integrity. All these things have I given willingly and with honest intent. And now I have seen with joy how willingly your people who are here have given to you. O Lord . . . keep this desire in the hearts of your people forever, and keep their hearts loyal to you. And give my son Solomon the wholehearted devotion to keep your commands" (1 Chronicles 29:17-19)*. David's keen awareness of God's influence on open hearts and willing minds is noteworthy here. In Solomon's case, regretfully, freewill clearly got the best of him.

Elsewhere, David writes: *"Search me, O God, and know my heart; test me and know my anxious thoughts. See if there is any offensive way in me, and lead me in the way everlasting" (Psalm 139:23-24).* In sincerely searching for God's will we not only find Him but ultimately find ourselves in the process. Soren Kierkegaard once remarked, "And, now, with God's help, I shall become myself." Colson writes, "We discover meaning and purpose, not in the search for self, but in surrender of self, in obedience to Christ" *(Colson, pp. 24-25).* Fortunately, since *"God is greater than our hearts" (1 John 3:20),* people often find Him whether they're seeking Him or not, though the choice is ultimately theirs to make. Thankfully, it was Jonah, not me, who ended up in the belly of a whale. I just ended up in Dubke, God's venue for giving me the *"desires of my heart,"* yet again, unequivocally demonstrating His divine sense of humor. No, God didn't do that by granting my every wish. In fact, He didn't give me anything I had ever consciously dreamt of having. As crazy as it sounds, though, He did something even better.

    I'm about to get weighty on you here so please bear with me for a couple of pages. I promise it'll be over before you know it. When many gloss over Psalm 37:4, *"Delight yourself in the Lord and he will give you the desires of your heart,"* they instinctively fancy some primitive version of a cuddly omnipotent genie answering our every prayer request with a resounding, "Hey, whatever it is, baby, you got it!" However, answering all of our petitions, many of which tend to be pretty egocentric, not to say self-destructive, aside from contradicting two-thirds of the Bible's content, would inevitably lead to disaster. Furthermore, a general word study opens up a whole new can of worms. In Psalm 37:4 the Hebrew word for *"give"* is *"<u>nathan</u>,"* carrying with it a mother-load of notable nuances. The *Enhanced Strong's Lexicon* reports that there are 2,008 occurrences of *"<u>nathan</u>" (reference # 5414)* in the Old Testament, offering voluminous potential meanings for the word. *"Give"* is the predominant rendering in the King James Version, with 1,078 usages throughout the context of the Old Testament. Psalm 37:4 happens to be an example in which the mysterious word *"give"* is rendered by the majority of English translations *(eBible Deluxe),* but the word *"give"* muddies the waters thanks to its ambiguity. That's because giving can mean many different things in varying circumstances.

The Russian version, unlike most English translations, confidently goes out on a limb by using the very explicative word *"fulfill,"* seemingly, to the casual reader, transforming one's faith into Aladdin's Lamp. We should all be so lucky! Suffice it to say that although the impression of *"grant"* or *"fulfill"* in Psalm 37:4 may have some support, some qualification, notwithstanding, is indispensable. If God has chosen to *"fulfill"* the desires of our hearts then it's only because our wishes are commensurate with His ultimate will. The first half of Psalm 37:4 is fundamental here: *"Delight yourself in the Lord."* It's only then that the desires of our hearts change enough to match the desires of His heart. Prior to Jesus' famous words, *"And I will do whatever you ask" (John 14:13)*, He prefaced that in the preceding verse with, *"Anyone who has faith in Me will do what I have been doing."* Let's always remember that no matter what Jesus did, whether that involved lounging in the shade or performing astounding miracles, He never once strayed from His prime aspiration of carrying out the desires of His Father's heart. So, while the *"grant"* or *"fulfill"* interpretation of *"nathan"* may present a possibility, let's also be cognizant of its mandatory conditions as well as the fact that there are several credible alternative meanings to *"nathan"* that shouldn't be overlooked.

Incidentally, although the *Enhanced Strong's Lexicon* fails to list *"fulfill"* as a general possibility for *"nathan,"* it does pose the word *"grant,"* denoting that same notion in this particular context. But, by the same token, it also shows how the literal rendering of *"grant"* is extremely rare, appearing just 21 times in the King James Version. Either way, it's understandable why almost all English translations use the word *"give"* in Psalm 37:4 because its vague neutrality fits our dusky context well. Parallel passages don't help much either. For example, Proverbs 10:24, a very similar verse, also makes use of *"nathan,"* but Psalm 20:4-5 raises questions by twice introducing us to another Hebrew word meaning *"to fulfill,"* which is *"mala"* (# 4390). Moreover, the context of Psalm 20:4-5 restricts us from drawing any solid conclusions regarding our discussion *(eBible Deluxe)*.

Cross-referencing the *Englishman's Concordance* with the *Enhanced Strong's Lexicon*, in light of the massive collection of English Bible translations, even in the book of Genesis alone, adds to the mire. In Genesis 3:6 "*nathan*" is used simply to describe how Eve "*gave*" the forbidden fruit to her husband. Likewise, God told Noah that all of the fish and animals were "*delivered*" into his hand *(Genesis 9:2)*, similar to Joseph being "*entrusted*" with all of Potiphar's possessions *(eBible Deluxe)*. Transferring one's possessions or handing a piece of fruit to somebody speaks for itself, without the need for any lengthy explanation. The desires of the heart, by contrast, as previously noted, are another matter altogether.

In Genesis 1:17, the word "*nathan*" is used to describe how God "*set*" or "*positioned*" the stars in the sky. Similar meanings can be seen in Genesis 15:10 where Abram "*arranged*" animal parts opposite each other or in Genesis 18:8 where he "*placed*" a meal before his three heavenly guests. So, rather than God "*fulfilling*" all of our hearts' desires, Psalm 37:4 might actually infer that He "*sets*" or "*arranges*" our hearts' desires according to their proper courses, like He did with the stars in the beginning. In other words, He takes our muddled priorities and revitalizes them by putting them in the appropriate order, which inescapably results in lasting joy.

"*Nathan*" is also used of the ground refusing to "*yield*" its crops in Genesis 4:12. Genesis 49:20 is comparable though English translations present populous renderings like "*produce*," "*provide*," "*grow*," and "*yield*," among others. With this rendering, David could be depicting how God "*produces*" our hearts' desires, or that He allows deeply suppressed, long forgotten, or buried wants, to resurface or sprout forth like crops from the ground. Again, we are reminded of David's prayer in 1 Chronicles 29:18-19: *"O Lord... keep this desire in the hearts of your people forever, and keep their hearts loyal to you. And give my son Solomon the wholehearted devotion to keep your commands."* Furthermore, in Genesis 9:12, God "*makes*" an agreement with Noah, again viably suggesting that God forms or creates our hearts' desires when we let Him *(eBible Deluxe)*.

"*Nathan*" further denotes the process of foreordaining, appointing, or establishing, as is evident from God's words to

Abram: *"Your name will be Abraham, for I have 'made' you the father of many nations" (Genesis 17:5)*. This facet of the word could convey the idea of God establishing our hearts' desires and choosing to work out His plan through them, as He did with Abraham. The Hebrew word also expresses the permitting or allowing of something, as Genesis 31:7 affirms. Additionally, Genesis 38:28 tells of how Zerah *"put out," "extended,"* or *"reached out"* his hand using "*nathan.*" This may symbolically illustrate how God extends or magnifies our hearts' desires. The act of *"storing"* something, or *"laying it up,"* is also inferred by the use of our Hebrew word in Genesis 41:48. Furthermore, implicit in our obscure Hebrew word is the aspect of *"assuming," "accusing,"* or *"believing to be the case,"* which is easily seen in Genesis 42:30 *(eBible Deluxe)*.

Before concluding our brief word study, let's not forget that *Vine's Complete Expository Dictionary of Old and New Testament Words* speaks of "*nathan*" appearing just a few chapters later. In Exodus 36:2, God "*placed*" into the hearts of the Hebrew craftsman the aptitude for using their God-given abilities, often typical of God's methodology *(eBible Deluxe)*. According to that passage they donated so much material that Moses had to officially request that they cease doing so. In this sense, parallel passages abound both in the Old and New Testaments. Concerning Lydia's conversion in Acts 16, Luke writes: *"The Lord opened her heart to respond to Paul's message" (v. 14)*. Another example is the case of Absalom, whose heart was absolutely unresponsive to true wisdom, in accordance with God's sovereign plan *(2 Samuel 17:14)*. Truly, the Great Optician's cardiology degree assuredly meets even the strictest standards of accreditation.

"Well, what's the verdict on Psalm 37:4?" you might ask. "What did David really intend to tell us?" I really wish David were here to give us a more convincing answer than mine. In fact, perhaps you know better than me. Although I can't tell you for sure, I do know that God never promises a rose garden. If you think He's going to handle all of your problems for you, or protect you from them, or constantly be at your beckoned call regardless of your circumstances or attitude, or offer you a green card to paradise on earth, then the land of downright disappointment is definitely where you're headed.

While the pessimist has a point in exclaiming that when things fall apart he's simply proved right, whereas when they don't he's pleasantly surprised, God never calls us to adopt that kind of attitude. He calls us, rather, to maintain a healthy psychological, theological, mental, and emotional balance, by being realistically optimistic.

David Ferguson also mentioned a psychiatric patient he once met. Her name is Sandy. After a drunk driver took the life of her husband, she was left with three small tots and a ton of grief. As a Christian woman, she determined to overcome her trials with firm conviction of faith, initially experiencing surprising success, all things considered. But things took a dramatic turn when she decided to get involved with her church's singles' ministry. Prior to doing so, many friends from her church carefully and consistently expressed concern for her, happily lending her a shoulder to cry on from time to time. They eagerly afforded her opportunities to vent her feelings of loneliness, confusion, and rage, encouraging the natural healing process to ensue while coupling it with supernatural solutions through prayer. Tragically, care and sensitivity were foreign concepts for her new acquaintances in the singles' ministry.

"How can you be lonely?" some yelped. "Don't you know you have God?"

Others made similar comments, "Lonely? That's not good! Maybe you need to see the pastor. A Christian doesn't need to feel lonely!" Self-condemnation accelerated into a suicide attempt inside of three months, leaving her more devastated and alone than she'd ever felt before *(Ferguson, pp. 53-54)*. This travesty just illustrates the fact that some Christians' souls weigh more than their brains, and I mean that in the negative sense. Admittedly, some professed believers aren't only spiritually deceased, but they're brain-dead too. Consequently, others suffer unduly all because some pinheaded churchgoers ironically act as though denying reality, as long as it's in Jesus' Name, is still acceptable.

The truth is that life isn't perfect and it never will be, no matter how much faith you have. Jesus Himself stated that God *"causes His sun to rise on the evil and the good, and sends rain on the righteous and the unrighteous" (Matthew 5:45)*. Jesus' renowned words in John 16:33, *"In this world you will have trouble,"* were spoken to His closest friends. In fact, most of them suffered more than the majority of us ever will, even culminating in martyrdom. Maybe you can relate to Paul, who requested that God relieve him of his annoying vexation three separate times, yet was denied. The answer he received certainly reminded him, as it does us, that the fulfillment derived from a close walk with God is more than enough to deliver contentment regardless of our circumstances: *"My grace is sufficient for you" (2 Corinthians 12:9).* Notice Paul's words in the following verse, *"That is why, for Christ's sake, I delight in weaknesses, in insults, in hardships, in persecutions, in difficulties."* And, for Christ's sake, so can we.

Suffering wasn't limited to the apostles though, for the writer of Psalm 37 also got his share of it. David, after displaying heroic faith in his confrontation with Goliath, his older brother's vicious condemnation notwithstanding, consequently fled for his life because of King Saul's jealous rage. So, just for one honorable deed, our shepherd boy became a fugitive for approximately fourteen long years. Adding to this, while on the run, David's life was also put in jeopardy in Gath by the servants of Achish. Thus, he was temporarily forced to feign insanity. In fact, this seemingly perpetually inequitable absconding scenario will later repeat itself when David's own son, Absalom, sets out to steal the throne by getting rid of papa. Withal, the king still wept bitterly upon hearing the news about Absalom's violent end. David also mourned over the murder of his son Amnon, who had been guilty of raping his own sister.

David's hardships had just begun, though, for coupled with his son's betrayal were other double-crossers. One of them was especially intriguing. While David was archetypal of Christ at times, David's eerie advisor, Ahithophel, prefigured Judas Iscariot. Ahithophel, akin to the infamous disciple, not only obtained apostle-like status *(2 Samuel 16:23)* but also plotted the demise of his former king after his master spent much time in prayer, contemplating imminent death, on the Mount of Olives *(2 Samuel 15:30-31; Luke 22:39).* According to 2 Samuel 15:31, while David was on the Mount of Olives, we see that he, being symbolic of the Lord Himself, was already made privy to his betrayer's intentions. We further notice that David's prayers on the Mount related to the traitor. If that parallel doesn't convince you then notice 2 Samuel 20, where all of the Israelites deserted David, exactly like Jesus' disciples did after His arrest.

Joab was another issue for David. As the commander of David's army, though occasionally displaying wisdom, he essentially turned out to be a royal thorn in the king's flesh by murdering Absalom against the king's wishes. Yet, David was subsequently unsuccessful in replacing him with Amasa because Joab in-turn mowed him down also, as recorded in 2 Samuel 20. Hence, Joab, David's leading general, failed to make David's Warrior Hall of Fame, in 2 Samuel 23, because he became a nasty sore for which the king had absolutely no remedy, even unto his dying day.

Incidentally, as a side note to our discussion, Uriah the Hittite curiously made that official warrior list, according to 2 Samuel 23:39. In fact, Uriah seems to stand out there because he's actually the final GI to round up the list. And what's significant here is that this listing immediately precedes the peculiar account of David's sinful census in the following chapter. There, in verse seventeen, we see David's confession of guilt concerning the census, backed by a self-sacrificial prayer regarding the slaying of the innocent. Although this prayer related directly to the victims of the census, it's probably also recorded directly after Uriah's honorable mention to show how David's role in the slaying of that innocent victim haunted him for decades. Even towards the end of chapter twenty-four we're reminded of the former consequences of that particular slaying, in David's personal life, by his words to Araunah, *"I will not sacrifice to the Lord my God burnt offerings that cost me nothing"* (*2 Samuel 24:24*). Either way, certainly Joab's killing of the innocent, including his direct involvement in Uriah's death, provided the king with an abundance of horrible memories and sleepless nights.

While this isn't a comprehensive list of David's hardships, it is sufficient to make a point: DAVID'S LIFE WAS NO PICNIC! Though somewhat debatable, the majority of these trials, if not all of them, occurred while David was walking closely with the Lord. Therefore, adducing that King David proposed an Aladdin's-Lamp view of Psalm 37:4 seems improbable because many of his prayer requests were met with a resonant, *"Not a chance my royal servant!"*

Nope, David seldom got all he wished for on a silver platter. As you know, God has at least six patented answers to prayer requests: 1) "Yes," 2) "Yes, but," 3) "No," 4) "No, but," 5) "Wait," and 6) "Are you out of your mind?" And a quick glance at the biblical account confirms that David received all six answers fairly evenly. By the same token, his unfolding evolvement as a godly leader into *"a man after God's own heart"* is especially visible whenever his trials served as the primary backdrop for his life and reign. In reading the Psalms, even the careless reader will see that David's cultivating maturity granted him a level of satisfaction that even his life's crosses couldn't swipe away.

Finally, let's take a look at the context of Psalm 37:4. Verses five and six set the tone: *"Commit your way to the Lord; trust in Him and He will do this: He will make your righteousness shine like the dawn, the justice of your cause like the noonday sun" (vv.5-6).* Immediately after mentioning the *"desires of your heart"* David elaborates by emphasizing God's true aim, which is enhancing our commitment to Him, our quest for righteousness, and our pursuit of justice. In other words, His ultimate desire is that you *"delight yourself in the Lord."* David persuades us not to envy the wicked, for although they may temporarily succeed in carrying out their ungodly desires, they still lack what really matters in life: *"Better the little that the righteous have than the wealth of many wicked; for the power of the wicked will be broken, but the Lord upholds the righteous...The Lord delights in the way of the man whose steps He has made firm; though he stumble, he will not fall, for the Lord upholds him with His hand... For the Lord loves the just and will not forsake His faithful ones...The mouth of the righteous man utters wisdom, and his tongue speaks what is just. The law of his God is in his heart; his feet do not slip" (vv.16-17, 23-24, 28, 30-31).* Notice that it is God who directs our steps by placing His law within our hearts. Perhaps that's why Psalm 119 reads: *"Blessed are they whose ways are blameless, who walk according to the law of the Lord. Blessed are they who keep His statutes and seek Him with all their heart...I seek you with all my heart; do not let me stray from your commands. I have hidden your word in my heart that I might not sin against you... I rejoice in following your statutes as one rejoices in great riches" (vv.1-2, 10-11, 14).* Simply put, our greatest desires can't even compare with the joy that God's desires, within our hearts, can offer us. The Psalmists, time and again, relay the very same message: there is no greater feeling on earth, available to humans, than the fulfillment that comes from a close relationship with our Creator.

Solomon asked for wisdom from the Lord and God's response is relevant here: *"Since you have asked for this and not for long life or wealth for yourself, nor have you asked for the death of your enemies but for discernment in administering justice, I will do what you have asked" (1 Kings 3:11-12).* Jesus said, *"Ask whatever you wish, and it will be given to you" (John 15:7),* but He couched those words in the context of remaining in Him by obeying His commands with a heart of love. He even preceded those words in verse seven with this condition: *"If you remain in me and my words remain in you."* The goal is making sure that our hearts' desires match His, allowing us to pray, aspire, and act, according to His perfect will. If that goal is met, then you can bet your bottom dollar that your prayers will be answered. In fact, God may even decide to bless you with some extra stuff, as He did in Solomon's case, reflecting the additional fringe benefits that often accompany this win-win relationship with Him.

For what it's worth, I believe that in giving us our hearts' desires, rather than granting us all we've ever wished for, God supplies all that we intrinsically need to become the people He intends for us to be. This is so that He can get closer to us than He's ever been before, in-turn fulfilling the underlying desire of His heart. "Yeah! Yeah! Okay, John, but how does all of this work?" you might ask. "Break this down for me, will you?" **Well, I firmly believe that when we finally get God's attention by attempting something extraordinary for Him, whatever that may mean for you in your situation, He supernaturally accomplishes this for us by taking a spiritual shovel and either planting brand spanking new and improved desires into our hearts, which formerly didn't exist there, or by taking a spiritual crowbar and prying our eyes open so we can see, for the first time ever, the healthiest tendencies already inside our hearts that we've callously ignored due to**

sin's deceitfulness, something we'll briefly touch on a bit later. In other words, when we deliberately step out of our normal lives to get His attention, He responds by stepping in to get ours. THE CRUX? Well, it actually happens to be those particular desires and inclinations that truly represent *God's perfect plan* for our lives, meaning that nothing else we decide to chase on this earth can deliver comparable dividends. So, hey, what are you waiting for?

In my case, God essentially gave me my real heart by finally enabling me to find my true self in Him, thanks to one small step in His direction: *A cross-cultural mission trip*. During those two short months He uncovered the hidden desires of my heart that would bring me unrivaled fulfillment in more ways than I had ever imagined before. He, at long last, helped me to see a much GRANDER and more *blessing-packed* direction than the one I had previously envisioned for myself. In the end, my heart, after a complete overhaul, finally found a special place within His. The Great Cardiologist helped me unmask the burden of my heart for the people of Ukraine, instilling in me a unique desire to serve them, and filling me with a peace that passes all understanding regarding that decision. He also touched my life with His providential activity in terms previously unfamiliar to me. It may be hard to explain but it's true. So, in delighting ourselves in Him, we successfully soften our calloused hearts in a way that allows God to enter them and bless our lives by becoming the Lord of our ambitions. The classic Christian rock band, Petra, put it perfectly on their album *Wake Up Call*: "Just reach out and He'll reach in."

Chapter Five
Confused and VERY far from home

Several years ago, we organized weekly gatherings at a Christian café in Crimea. It was generally a cultural program that we were designing in order to get better acquainted with members of the Tatar community. We often played games while binging on wads of refreshments. One specific game involved scribbling down Bible verses on small pieces of paper. Then, on another piece, we'd jot down something we'd always wanted to do but just never had the chance to do. We'd later mix up the pile, pick from the hat, and read whatever ended up in our hands. I once wrote that I wanted to jump out of an airplane, which got matched up with, *"Because the truth will set you free."* Well, in John 8:32 Jesus did say, *"And you shall know the truth and the truth will set you free" (NASB)*, but I doubt that jumping out of an airplane was quite what He had in mind. In verse 34, Christ added, *"I tell you the truth, everyone who sins is a slave to sin."* Today, I heartily confess that I'm living proof of those words because it wasn't until I ventured out of my own will, for once in my life, that this slave to sin was released by the power of His truth. Praise God! Jesus' famous phrase, *"He who has ears to hear, let him hear" (Mark 4:9)*, really hit home. And this man will never be the same again.

In 1 Samuel 10, the prophet Samuel anoints Israel's first king. His name was Saul. Just in the previous chapter, though, we see Saul searching for some of his Dad's stray donkeys with a servant from his father's household, which was basically his primary goal in life at that particular moment. Surely, even in his wildest dreams, he couldn't have predicted that instead of finding those mules he'd find the most powerful seat in the land. But that's not all he found. Amid their first meeting, the prophet both discloses the fact that Dad's donkeys have been located *(9:20)* and continues to inform Saul of his plans for the following day: *"I will...tell you all that is in your heart" (9:19)*. Well, that's definitely one of God's specialties. And sometimes He does that gradually, while at other times, He just hits us right between the eyes. Saul evidently got the latter and therefore wasn't quite ready to respond. Even on the day of his scheduled coronation, Saul is found hiding out *(10:22)*. Yet, after getting a tiny taste of power he eventually slipped into his role rather eagerly. The fact is that when God opens your heart with His unmitigated truth you never know where you'll end up or how you got there, but you'll ultimately be exhilarated beyond words whenever you finally arrive. The key is getting there, whatever that might mean for you personally. The reason? We'll let Jesus explain that one: *"If the Son sets you free, you will be free indeed" (John 8:36)*. However, that freedom usually doesn't come effortlessly.

James, in his first chapter, mentions the *"word of truth,"* which generally seems to be the central focus there *(v. 18)*. He even gives us a few practical tips on how to understand that *"word of truth."* In verse 21, he encourages us to *"accept the word planted in you."* The problem, though, is that we'll never be able to unless we're willing to do so wholeheartedly. James continues in verse twenty-one by exhorting us to *"get rid of all moral filth."* Interestingly enough, the Greek word for *"filth"* there literally has a dual meaning. If you've ever changed a diaper then you can certainly speculate as to the general meaning, but in medicinal terms it can also refer to "ear wax." So James firmly acknowledges that continually doing whatever feels good at the moment, without considering God's desires, hinders one from developing any practical understanding of God's word. Sin's deceitful desires cause spiritual deafness. Thus, coupled with the emptiness of a sinful lifestyle, the devil offers us spiritual cataracts and bushels of spiritual potatoes with which to clog up our ears. What more could we ask for? In Dubke, by the way, I found all kinds of spiritual and physical potatoes. In fact, I probably gobbled down more potatoes that summer than I'd eaten in the previous five years of my life. Nevertheless, God used that potato-packed village to eliminate my spiritual spuds so that His voice could finally ring out in digital Dolby surround-sound for the first time ever. Even Paul's words, in 1 Corinthians 14:25, started making sense to me. Though the context differed from my situation, there were similar results. Look at how Paul describes what happens to the unbeliever who gets convicted by God's Spirit: *"And the secrets of his heart will be laid bare. So he will fall down and worship God."*

Cincinnati Bible Seminary differed from Dubke in at least two ways: 1) no Muslims, and 2) all the running water you ever needed. Yet, they both had something in common. Just as my seminary education was like nursery school in the real world, my new figurative heart transplant was merely the beginning of a new spiritual perspective and relationship with God. I still had lots of questions and very few answers. Although I realized that I had a new heart with a crazy new outlook, it was still a mystery to me. Our hearts are a lot like onions because as the layers are peeled away there's always bound to be lots of wide eyes and tears. Ezekiel described how God would replace Israel's calloused hearts with soft ones that would be inspired by His Spirit to move in His direction instead of their own *(Ezekiel 36:25 ff)*. Paul alluded to Christian Baptism as the moment when a person's heart is circumcised by faith and repentance *(Colossians 2:11 ff)*, in fulfillment of the prophets' words, but Jeremiah still had this to say: *"The heart is deceitful above all things and beyond cure. Who can understand it? 'I the Lord search the heart and examine the mind, to reward a man according to his conduct, according to what his deeds deserve'" (17:9-10)*. Even Paul claimed ignorance regarding his heart: *"Indeed, I do not even judge myself. My conscience is clear, but that does not make me innocent. It is the Lord who judges me" (1 Corinthians 4:3-4)*. Scripture even indicates that God Himself occasionally does a little investigating regarding the secret matters of the heart. Concerning

King Hezekiah, we see these words: *"God left him to test him and to know everything that was in his heart" (2 Chronicles 32:31)*. So, if even the Lord researches the heart at times, how can any human being begin to uncover its mysteries? God alone possesses both an unadulterated knowledge of the contents of each person's heart as well as perfect insight into the true needs and desires of every single individual. Hence, while Paul's eyes were certainly wide open, that didn't mean that all of his questions had been answered. He still had to trust and obey like the rest of us. So, though we've uncovered one effective formula that God uses to open the eyes of our hearts, let's remember that there's a catch: it's not a two-month process, but a lifetime process.

Immediately after the internship, while standing on my parents' doorstep, still holding my suitcase, I was greeted with hugs and kisses and excitement and joy and all things good. "He's back," they shouted. "We thought you'd never return."

"Well," I replied, "I'm not totally sure how to put this but my return is only temporary."

"What do you mean?" Mom asked.

"Well, I'm going back," I replied.

"Ah, I see," Mom sighed. "Are you going back this second, or do you want to come inside and grab a bite to eat first?" Incidentally, after savoring Mom's scrumptious cooking, I feasted on a daily dose of humble pie for quite a while. My new day timer had lots of penitent self-examination hours scheduled. Francis Frangipane, in his book *The Three Battlegrounds*, described my case flawlessly: "There is a difference between repenting for a sin and actually pulling down the stronghold within us that produced the sin. The first involves faith in the cross of Christ; the second demands we embrace crucifixion ourselves" *(1989, p. 111)*. It's not only repentance for a particular sin that many of us need; it's also repentance for the whole attitude that initially led us to that specific point in our lives. It's that oppressive system of thinking, which has so firmly established itself within our hearts and minds over the years, that we must sincerely confront most of all *(see Romans 12:1-2, and Ephesians 4:23.)*

"Cathy" is a famous comic strip. And one particular episode shows the consequences of entertaining a tempting thought instead of dismissing it immediately. Cathy was battling her desire to break the rules of her diet and the captions displayed her unchecked thoughts, which are prone to sweeping us away when we're not careful.

The first frame read: "I'll take a drive, but I won't go near the grocery store."

Frame two read: "I'll drive by, but I won't go in."

Frame three: "I'll go into the grocery store but I won't walk down the aisle where the Halloween candy is."

Frame four: "I'll look at the candy, but I won't pick it up."

Frame five: "I'll pick it up, but I won't buy it."

Frame six: "I'll buy it, but I won't open it."

Frame seven: "Open it, but won't smell it."

Frame eight: "Smell it, but won't taste it."

Frame nine: "Taste it, but won't eat it."

Frame ten: "Eat, eat, eat, eat, eat, eat."

In 1 Corinthians 10:13, Paul reminds us that God provides a way of escaping each and every kind of temptation but we need to remember that the best escape route is in the first frame. Cathy lost both the battle and the war when she decided to take that drive. And if we don't continually control ourselves in the first frame then Satan will get a grip on our lives and botch them up royally. Now, let's all understand that frame number one in our lives is really our thinking. Francis Frangipane continues: "Jesus was crucified in the place of the skull, and we too must be crucified there daily. It's the realm of our thought life." But being *transformed by the renewing of our minds" (Romans 12:2)* is no small task.

In Matthew 12, Jesus confronted the Jewish leaders who were asking for a sign of His authority. Their minds were pad-locked. In fact, earlier in the chapter they had concluded that Jesus was possessed because, in reality, their minds actually were. Jesus told them, *"When an evil spirit comes out of a man, it goes through arid places seeking rest and doesn't find it. Then it says, 'I will return to the house I left.' When it arrives, it finds the house unoccupied, swept clean and put in order. Then it goes and takes with it seven other spirits more wicked than itself and they go in and live there. And the final condition of that man is worse than the first" (vv. 43-45).* Here,

Jesus plainly states that demons find rest within our lives when our thought lives are off-track. It's that scary and it's that simple!

In 2 Corinthians 10:1-5, Paul speaks of *"strongholds"* in the Church. Paul reminds us that there's a spiritual war going on and our minds are the battlefield. It is a war with our minds hanging in the balance. And we need to realize that strongholds are sinful or destructive thought patterns that Satan has successfully planted within our minds, whether it's the result of habits he helped us form, interaction with people through whom he's operating, direct demonic influence, or circumstances he's responsible for, among other means. Strongholds may consist of evil or sinful thoughts, as well as untruths leading to all kinds of deception. Consequences range from falling prey to false doctrines to even the development of psychological disorders, since many mental illnesses are primarily based on misconceptions and irrational fears within our minds. Just as sin deceives our consciences by conning us into doing things that we know we shouldn't do, psychological disorders deceive our minds into believing things we know we shouldn't believe. Though we know it's wrong, we still do it. And though we know it's not true, we still believe it. And that's the irony of sin. Hebrews 3:12-13 advises us: *"See to it, brothers, that none of you has a sinful, unbelieving heart that turns away from the living God. But encourage one another daily...so that none of you may be hardened by sin's deceitfulness."* We can either open our minds to the devil's influence, letting him both deceive us and control our very thoughts, or we can experience freedom and victory in Jesus Christ.

Paul, in 2 Corinthians 10:4, displays the impracticality of outwitting the devil in this battle for our minds. Our own human efforts will never succeed no matter how disciplined or cunning we accredit ourselves as being. In fact, that false confidence many seem to have is actually a great example of a stronghold. Rather, our weapons need to have *"divine power to demolish strongholds."* They are the only weapons that prove effective, though many believers have all but given up on them because they fail to witness or grasp their true efficacy. Their ailing vision is simply a result of Satan's strongholds already having established themselves within their minds. Weapons that have *"divine power"* are the ones we are all well acquainted with:

love, prayer, fasting, Bible study, worship, meditation on Scripture, evangelism, fellowship with believers, obedience to Christ, and genuine saving faith *(see James 2)*. Generally speaking, it's the full armor of God *(see Ephesians 6)* and the fruit of the Spirit *(see Galatians 5:22ff)*. We all know about these weapons, but if we're not using them then rest assured that Satan is rapidly advancing in the battle for our minds. Only a close walk in the truth with Jesus Christ can pave an unparalleled path to genuine release.

Literally examining Paul's use of the word *"thoughts"* (<u>noema</u>) in 2 Corinthians is helpful because it subtly hints at how involved Satan really is in this battle for our minds. In 2 Corinthians 3:14 and 4:3-4, Paul explains that spiritual blindness is a result of Satan's activity in people's minds, using the word "<u>noema</u>" to refer to their thoughts or minds. Notice what he says about the unbelieving Jews: *"But their minds were made dull, for to this day the same veil remains when the old covenant is read."* So Satan was having his way with their minds even though they were hearing the Scriptures often. In chapter four, verse four, he writes, *"The god of this age has blinded the minds (<u>noema</u>) of unbelievers, so that they can't see the light of the gospel."* In 2 Corinthians 10:5, Paul writes, *"We take every thought (<u>noema</u>) captive to the obedience of Christ"* (NASB). He continues in 2 Corinthians 11:3, *"But I am afraid that just as Eve was deceived by the serpent's cunning, your minds (<u>noema</u>) may somehow be led astray from your sincere and pure devotion to Christ."* See, that's how Satan operates. Little by little, and very subtly, he works in our minds, convincing us that our thoughts are really our thoughts until we're rendered spiritually stagnant.

Statistics supposedly indicate that the majority of American congregations are stagnant. Allegedly, they are neither growing nor are they really making much of a difference in their communities. Robert Lewis points out that only a third of American ministers believe that the American Church is making a positive impact on the culture *(Lewis, p. 23)*. If that's really the case then Paul's point here probably hits the nail on the head: STRONGHOLDS. Perhaps Satan has the American Church wrapped around his pinky to the point that many even believe that spiritual stagnation is acceptable. Maybe it's time to start asking ourselves some tough questions.

Who are we really serving? Who really is winning the battle for our minds? Notice what Paul says about the devil in 2 Corinthians 2:11, *"For we are not unaware of his **schemes** (noema)."* Unfortunately, for many that's not entirely the case. Moreover, Paul repeatedly uses the Greek word "noema" to refer to our thoughts and minds in 2 Corinthians and, incredibly, he also uses that same Greek word when alluding to Satan's *"schemes."* Isn't it frightening to consider how intimately connected our minds are with the carrying out of Satan's plans?

All of us know that Satan is the *"Father of Lies" (John 8:44)*, but we often forget that he's lying to us too. And, like the Corinthians, we tend to forget that only God Himself is strong enough to do something about that. According to 1 Corinthians 1, they had been blessed with every spiritual gift imaginable. Strangely, though, they also had divisions resulting in lawsuits, spiritual arrogance stemming from the miraculous gifts themselves, heresies regarding the resurrection, disrespect for leaders, and immorality, all in concert with their rejection of Paul's authority. The Corinthians met each Sunday to break bread and worship Jesus like most of us do. Their minds, however, unbeknownst to them, were also being ravished by the devil. And before long they were drifting wholly outside the will of God. Some were even dying due to their spiritual rebellion *(see 1 Corinthians 11:30)*. And, as much as I hated to admit it, my first twenty-three years on the planet hadn't been much different. Thanks to the strongholds that were formerly holding my mind and heart captive, I failed to see the big picture. I failed to realize that my will essentially mattered more to me than God's. While Jesus was living proof that *"all things are possible with God" (Mark 10:27)*, I was living proof that just about all things are possible without Him. All things, that is, except rediscovering Him without His help. Like the Prodigal Son, I had somehow strayed entirely too far from home to make it back alone. But like the Prodigal I, too, fortunately hit rock bottom hard enough to see my fallen state.

Chapter Six
Refueling, Repairing, and Repenting

❦

Georges, my missionary friend in Crimea, organizes Christian symposiums there twice a year. They're conferences on ethics and morality in various fields, ranging from political science to biochemistry to psychology to theology. A few years ago, I recall how Georges was still working on his presentation just days before the conference. "Georges," I gibed, "are you still working on your paper?"

"Yeah!" he fussed. "I'm in charge of the conference and my project happens to be the only one that hasn't been handed in yet."

"What's it called?" I asked.

"Believe it or not," he quipped, "it's called 'The Myth of Progress,' but the real myth is that I'm actually making progress on it." Well, after the internship, when I began climbing the highest peak in the universe, Mt. Repentance, I could certainly empathize. There were days when I felt that progress would be next to impossible but God still led the way.

While living in Dubke, I once left home and walked through the garden on my way to the bus stop, completely forgetting about our new fence. So I had to turn around and take a detour. Then I got down the road and realized that I totally forgot my cash. Then, when

I finally got into the city, I realized that I had forgotten the medicines I was supposed to bring to a specific family I was visiting that day. What a day! What a dope! Likewise, there were similar days on this new road to spiritual recovery; loads of hurdles, a few detours along the way, and frustration galore. Then again, had it been easy, I wouldn't have needed God like I did, which was His main point. "Man's extremity," as they say, "is God's opportunity."

I'll never forget that drunk on the Ukrainian bus who happened to be bleeding all over the place. A nasty cut opened up over his eye and he bled all over the lady who was checking for tickets. In fact, his blood was dripping all down her arm. In America there would have been sheer hysteria, but, for some strange reason, not in this new place. Similarly, although my healing process was painful and even hectic at times, there was still a weird sense of peace about it that kept me afloat. True, the doggy-paddle was just about all I could muster, but sometimes it's the slowest results that stick the best.

In any case, I had ridden some great roller coasters before but this one took the cake. Even our group's grand exit from Ukraine that summer was preceded by a lifelong-impression-making-this-can-only-happen-in-Ukraine episode that went straight into my journal that very night. Prior to our scheduled departure from Kiev, on the following day, our group spent the night in two separate apartments located in the same building. The girls stayed with the owners in their furnished flat while the guys stayed in their other unfurnished apartment that had been vacant for months. Well, after yapping away until midnight, I made my way down to the male abode where almost everyone seemed to be sound asleep. Grinning in the dark, after finding a small void on the lone double bed in the living room, I thought I had lucked out since almost everyone else got the floor. Well, my grin faded fast; shut-eye wouldn't be in the cards that night. Like a married couple, the two of us on that bed battled for rights to the only sheet available. Besides, it was our only protection from the night; our only shield from the dark; our only hope against...that horde of killer mosquitoes swarming all over that dreadful corridor of pain and suffering. Yep, these were the demon-possessed mosquitoes Beth Miller had warned us about. Since that flat had no screens on any of its windows, as predicted, and because it had been unoccupied for so long, it was just infested by a wide variety of organic life forms. Welcome to the jungle . . . in Kiev of all places!

Well, since we had such a long journey scheduled for the following day, we had no choice but to face them head on, fighting tooth and claw to survive...and get some rest too. Since I was preoccupied almost to the verge of insanity by slapping myself in the face every three to four seconds, I initially figured that I was the only soldier fighting this war. It's not that nobody else was writhing in misery; it's just that I was way too distracted to notice. Anyway, I vainly kept hoping against hope that this nightmare would pass from me. It didn't. So, after about two hours of squirming in agony I finally decided to give up and get up. So I frantically sat up in the bed thinking, "Why me Lord? WHY?" Just then, our leader, Marty, who had been lying on the floor, also sat up. His look of horror, expressing even more than my own, told me that I was not alone on the battlefield. After three hours on the floor in that apartment, he had won the right to be called "the real-deal," a bona fide veteran leader who had fully earned his medals that night. All that, notwithstanding, after staring at this wounded soldier for just a few seconds he broke. "It's happened!" he whined. "We're in hell!"

It wasn't long before all of us guys were running around outside in our Underroos because when we strolled into the kitchen, we discovered that the floor was literally moving. Despite the roaches going all out with a super-groovy disco ball combined with their laser-light show, we chose not to hang around very long. A line from my journal entry that night should help, "I'm fairly confident that the Battle of Armageddon will occur between the roaches and the mosquitoes in this apartment. I'm just not sure yet who will win." Please do excuse the far-fetched theology there, but let's not forget to factor in that temporary insanity thing.

Well, there you have it: the end of just the beginning of John's many escapades in the former USSR. So, please sit back, relax, and enjoy, because our journey is far from over. Moses wrote, in Deuteronomy 4:29, *"If...you seek the Lord your God, you will find Him if you look for Him with all your heart and with all your soul."* Comparable to Psalms 37:4 was my evolving understanding of that particular verse on a fresh new level. But that new outlook neither excluded temporary spells of spiritual stupidity *(immaturity)* mixed with adult-sized temper tantrums *(selfishness)*, nor did it mean that merely sunshine and smooth sailing lay on the horizon. Giving every portion of our hearts to God is not only a very lengthy process, but it usually increases the intensity of life's challenges. Our satisfaction is that God's perspective never fails to manufacture genuine contentment no matter what happens. For the spiritually mature that outlook often comes natural, but the rest of us usually need frequent reminders.

Dobson tells of how Sandra Lund's family stayed in a local shelter while Hurricane Andrew wreaked havoc in South Florida a few years back. Upon returning to her demolished home the following day, Sandra experienced a flood of emotions while rummaging through the dregs. In her former kitchen, she recognized that the note she'd written to herself flawlessly weathered the storm. In it she quoted Paul's words in Philippians 4:11-12, *"I am not saying this because I am in need, for I have learned to be content whatever the circumstances...I have learned the secret of being content in any and every situation."* That's surely a reminder that'll stick with her for some time to come *(Dobson, p. 127)*.

As for Paul, these weren't just empty words because he wrote them from his prison cell. Ironically, still, while Paul may have been locked up, his sense of release in the Lord Jesus was inalienable. And although I'll probably never achieve quite that level of inner peace, I will say that some of God's lessons in a subsequent chapter of my life would at least bring me one step closer to it.

Part Two:
Strange Country? Dumb American?

Chapter Seven
My first real whiff

It's fascinating how we become more acutely aware of Satan's opposition after deciding to fully submit to God's will for our lives. It's also interesting to see how opposition can crop up anywhere. Even Jesus failed to escape temptation while fasting in the middle of nowhere before launching His public ministry. Several years ago, in New York I ran into a wealthy and rather obnoxious relative of my brother-in-law's. "Yeah, I hear you're going to Ukraine to help people," he sneered. "Why would you go all the way over there to help those jerks out? You should be helping us instead!"

"You know, maybe you're right," I snickered, "there are lots of jerks here who also need assistance. What can I do for you?" Fortunately, having been a New Yorker myself, I also tended to have my obnoxious moments periodically. I remember riding on the trolleybus in Ukraine when a crowd inadvertently nudged me into an elderly woman. The bus was so crowded that contact with at least three people at a time was inevitable. In fact, if that's all the contact you had then you were lucky. Nevertheless, the elderly woman scowled and raised her voice at me. BIG MISTAKE! I just looked at her and made one of those how-dare-you faces, which apparently didn't affect her much.

"Mya, mya, mya, mya!" I snarled. "Mya, mya-mya-mya-mya!" I continued, even though the meaning of that was a mystery to both of us.

"What the heck?" she muttered, raising her eyebrows.

"Mya, mya, mya-mya-mya-mya!" I cried, continuing to make my extremely valid point. Either way, though she didn't care to keep our intriguing dialogue alive, her facial expression said more than enough. I guess the moral of the story is that our fiercest opposition usually comes from within, as James relays in his first chapter. Paul reminded the Corinthians of the example he set for them: *"When we are cursed, we bless; when we are persecuted, we endure it; when we are slandered, we answer kindly"* (1 Corinthians 4:12-13). Sadly, even in the process of surrendering to God, we often have more in common with His nemesis. Then again, I seriously doubt that even Lucifer himself understood what "Mya, mya, mya-mya!" meant.

Actually, when I first returned to Ukraine as a full-time missionary, although my surname is Murphy, my Russian visa read, "Morfy." Let's put it this way: "Bummer of a birthmark!" "Morfy" is literally the root word for "Morphine" in Russian. "Morfy, huh?" the customs officer chuckled. "Got any on you?" I'm sure my new elderly lady friend on the trolleybus also wondered about that possibility, which might just explain what happened next. While walking home one night, I was greeted by a man on the street who knew my name. I couldn't remember him to save my life, but after pretending like he was a distant relative of mine, during our short conversation, within five minutes yet another stranger approached me and did the same thing.

"Hey John," he whispered, "if you run into any problems at all, just let me know. I got your back!"

Stunningly, three minutes later a third complete stranger greeted me by name. I felt like I was on Ukrainian Candid Camera or something. Triple whammy. It's like when three of my friends were hanging out together and couldn't tell someone the time because all three of their watches had stopped. But that was a total fluke; these shady characters evidently were much more than that. And it definitely raised my anxiety level just a hair. "Hey John, how's the ministry going?" he asked.

"How do you know who I am?" I asked.

"Well," he explained, "talk on the street gets around, my American friend." "Oh, and by the way," he added, "the police know you and I happen to know them." Gee, that was reassuring! After inviting me to his café, he proceeded to slander both America and Americans even though his grandmother is a Virginia resident. Believe me, without totally becoming a traitor to my race, I valiantly sought out every opportunity to agree with him as much as humanly possible.

Sometime later, I entered an audio-video store to inquire about available mini-disc players. The clerk immediately replied, "John Morfy, right?"

"How do you know that?" I stammered.

"Oh, that's not important," he answered.

"No, really," I begged, "how?"

"I just know," he replied.

"Okay, alright," I sighed, "forget I even asked."

See, with a name like "Morfy," keeping a low profile in this strange new place wasn't the easiest assignment ever given. In fact, after moving in with the same family in Dubke again, it wasn't long before I was forced to move back into the city. The KGB claimed that it was "dangerous" living in a Muslim village. "Besides, it's only for your protection," they assured me. But since I was such a celebrity, living in an inconvenient spot without a phone or internet access, I was a bit skeptical of their motives.

All of this reminds me of an incident that occurred three months after returning to Ukraine. My friend, who was a university student, was scheduled to work at a collective farm for a month. This was mandatory for anyone getting a free education. Arriving at the train station a bit late, I knew time was fleeting, so I asked, "How much time do we have before the train leaves?" I really wanted to help my friend with her luggage but not enough to risk stepping onto the commuter train and having the doors close behind me.

"Oh, about ten minutes or so," she calmly persuaded. Well, exactly what I didn't want to occur happened. As I muscled the doors open, one of her friends pulled a lever to stop the train, just in time for my acrobatic exit. Immediately, two enraged policemen pounced on me with a nightstick, some cuffs, and tons of Russian attitude. One of them, who gladly dished me out a knee to the back, while I was lying facedown on the concrete, even stuck his finger in my mouth and fish-hooked me good *(pulled my right cheek back in order to control any head movements)*, just before cuffing me. Let's just say that they got my undivided attention in record time.

After lifting me to my feet they shouted, "What's your name?"
"John," I mumbled.
"Who?" they screamed.
"My name is John; I'm an American," I explained. My limited Russian, the fury at the precinct, the fact that I wasn't carrying my passport, and the semblance of a solitary confinement cell directly opposite me, all contributed to my undue level of stress. In time, the chief arrived and released me with a warning. So God showed up just in time. And, for that, although I was anything but enamored with the idea, I subsequently chose to return to the station with a stack of Bibles for the crew.

Since that reaction seems a tad better than shouting, "Mya-mya-mya-mya!" I sure wish I could say that Paul's example had successfully rubbed off on me. But the fact that we were talking about ten wrathful cops with clubs as opposed to a single elderly woman on the bus casts serious doubt on that particular hypothesis. Furthermore, if the truth be told, the infamous "Mya-mya" incident actually occurred at a later date, practically solidifying the case. Either way, submitting to God's will won't protect us from potential disaster, temptation, or spiritual warfare. In fact, the opposite is oft the case because God's will customarily remains at the center of the battlefield. Yet, that feeling of indescribable peace steadily lingers because, as I said earlier, that's precisely where He's at.

Some of my favorite verses in the Bible come from David's confrontation with Goliath. A puny shepherd boy without any formal combat training, without a sword or armor, and without the support of his family, still defeated a nine-foot killing machine because of a faithful perspective that wouldn't quit despite the odds: *"You come against me with sword and spear and javelin, but I come against you in the name of the Lord Almighty, the God of the armies of Israel, whom you have defied. This day the Lord will hand you over to me and I will strike you down... the whole world will know that there is a God in Israel. All those gathered here will know that it is not by sword or spear that the Lord saves; for the battle is the Lord's"* (1 Samuel 17:45-47). It's only when we willingly step into God's neighborhood that He offers us that same perspective. You see, David's secret weapon was neither a sling nor a stone, it was a daily walk in the presence of the living God: *"Even though I walk through the valley of the shadow of death, I will fear no evil, for you are with me" (Psalms 23:4).*

"Oh sure," many suppose, "those biblical examples are just nifty, but they don't really apply to people like me in the twenty-first century." Lance Armstrong would beg to differ. Most people who follow sports know that Armstrong is one of the greatest athletes in the world, but they may not be aware that he is also one of the greatest in history because of the struggles he has overcome. In 1996, Armstrong was diagnosed with cancer that subsequently spread to his abdomen, lungs, and brain, resulting in twelve weeks of chemotherapy and two operations, one of which was brain surgery. Everyone, except Armstrong, swore he was finished. Lance proceeded to ride his bike between 30 and 50 miles a day, in between chemo treatments, eventually attaining the Tour de France crown within three years' time. Nike even called him, "The first dead man to win the Tour de France." My advice is to take his advice, "If you ever get a second chance in life for something, go all the way!" Luckily for us, our God is a God of second chances. If we adopt His perspective, faithfully relying on Him in His presence and on His terms, then even the impossible becomes possible.

I sort of empathized with Armstrong. Regrettably, it was more because of his setbacks than his victories. Mine just happened to be more spiritual than physical. After becoming a full-time missionary, I was asked to speak to the students at my alma mater, many of whom didn't know me at that point. I also decided to use a cane as an object lesson, soliciting sundry looks of concern from all of my former professors. I told the kids that I went on my first mission trip as a handicapped person, where God miraculously healed me.

As you can imagine, when I set the cane aside there were many astonished faces. I proceeded to explain that, before the trip, I had always falsely assumed that I wasn't mission-field material. Even as a child, I considered missionaries to be spiritual superheroes, far more sacrificial than I ever was or had ever cared to be. But God used a mission trip to help me perceive things in a whole different light, releasing me from the limitations that I, with the devil's help, had placed on myself. Paul writes, *"Our competence comes from God. He has made us competent as ministers of a new covenant" (2 Corinthians 3:5-6)*. Nevertheless, my imperfect life perfectly illustrated the vast gulf separating competence from preparedness.

Somebody commented that, "If India were the most religious nation in the world and Sweden the least religious, then America is a bunch of Indians ruled by Swedes." Reformed Judaism has even been likened to America's Democratic Party with holidays, neither of them gaining much ground from that compliment. Syndicated American columnist, Mona Charen, reporting on America's Democratic Party, cited its infamous claim, "We have nothing to fear but fear itself!" Then she argued that it's more like, "We have nothing to offer but fear itself!" The Republican Party isn't much better these days. Mona even described her short exchange with a native-born African cabby in New York City who's planning to escape back to Africa as soon as possible because he doesn't want his children exposed to what American children digest daily. Sounds fitting for a land where, in 1991, the Pennsylvania Supreme Court reversed a decision against a convicted murderer simply because the prosecuting attorney happened to quote the Bible in the courtroom. Similarly, in Houston, Texas, a woman got an official visit from the police department just for distributing a few Christian tracts along with the candy she offered the children on Halloween. In fact, John Whitehead, of the Rutherford Institute, a Christian legal organization, wrote a 300-page book entitled *Religious Apartheid*, detailing myriad analogous examples of modern American injustice perpetrated against Christendom. Peter Marshall appropriately queried: "Do our leaders fear the public opinion polls or do they fear God Almighty?" While that might be a good question, I don't think many of us are too fond of the obvious answer.

It's no wonder that Bob Shannon, an American minister who visited Eastern Europe several years back, maintains that, spiritually speaking, modern America is located somewhere in the book of Revelation whereas Eastern Europe currently resides in the book of Acts. Although I generally agree with him, my initial impression was that most things in this strange country were more like the book of Revelation because they were practically incomprehensible to me. I'm sure that the Russians felt the same way about me though. If they didn't yet, then it was only a matter of time before they would. If you've ever worked directly with the American military then you might be able to grasp what I'm saying. So much seemed to go against the grain of whatever seemed remotely logical. In Arabic cultures, it's appropriate to get almost face to face with others while conversing, which is especially the case after a meal so others can smell the garlic on your breath. That's why the old Englishman and the Arabic scholar, during their brief conversation, covered the whole hallway while supposedly standing still. As expected, I'd heard similar stories like that regarding other cultures. I knew that cultures were different because of various beliefs, mentalities, and circumstances, among other things, but reading about them isn't quite the same as smelling them with your own nose.

Chapter Eight
First lasting impressions

One thing I wasn't adequately prepared for was the general mentality of many in this strange new world. I learned that under Communism there were no credible philosophy departments. Famous philosophers were hardly ever mentioned, which baffled my mind because of my interest in that field. When any of them were brought up, they were all categorically branded as devout atheists. Examples even went so far as to include Pascal and Newton. The Communists' position negated any special need for philosophy since atheism was all that supposedly existed. A Ukrainian friend named Anya reported that, under Communism, sex was another forbidden topic. In fact, it wasn't even referred to as something married couples did. It was generally described as something relating to animal instincts. Anya said that when she was in school the doctor would routinely perform physicals on all the female students to see which of them had previously engaged in sexual relations, subsequently posting their names up on a list in the hallway for all interested passersby. I guess that would eliminate the need for gossip in school but "humiliating" doesn't even begin to describe how they must have felt. All of that actually went on, ironically, within a system lacking any true basis for morality in the first place. To say that I was dumbfounded would be an understatement, regardless of modern America's eccentricity.

The misrepresentation of philosophy and other fields in the USSR undeniably led not only to the denial of reality but also to the birth of many strange ideas. In 1994, I remember being invited to a specific gathering of folks who were studying Esperanto, which is not only the longest lasting manmade universal language, but is also spoken by approximately eight million people worldwide. Having been originally invented by a Polish doctor named Ludovic Zamenhof, in 1887, philologists suggest that it is five times easier to learn than English and ten times easier than learning Russian. Leo Tolstoy supposedly became fluent in less than a day *(Brownell, p. 7)*. Well, this group was gathering for the purpose of facilitating peace and unity throughout the world, which Esperanto would supposedly help foster, as well as seeking inner peace and fulfillment through some mathematical formula they were ardently constructing. Naturally, neither the concept of finding happiness through a bunch of fractions and figures added up to me, nor did their invitation of a Christian minister make much sense. Perhaps it was just one way of showing their openness to new ideas or maybe they were thinking that Christian theologians had a few fractions of their own. I originally planned to speak for several minutes until I learned more about their peculiar principals, which convinced me to drastically shorten my speech since my math was a bit rusty. In fact, I only spoke for about two minutes. About the time I got finished introducing myself, I concluded with an extremely knotty formula of my own. It was so complicated that the whole group, before their thundering applause, rubbed their chins, appearing to be very deep-in-thought, and replied, "Wow! Thank you so much! That was very thought provoking! Sir, we want to thank you so much for coming today because you have, indeed, given us a lot to consider!"

Well, since you're dying to know the details, here's the gist and almost the entirety of my lengthy discourse: "Jesus plus you equals fulfillment!" Well, okay, not very deep, but true! In case you haven't noticed, math was never one of my strongest subjects.

That reminds me of a Russian man who came down to Crimea in order to present a paper at one of the symposiums I mentioned earlier. Due to the fact that there were many foreign contributors, his presentation was translated into English for international consideration and interaction, but he didn't get much positive feedback, sad to say, since he lost the majority of foreigners within the first three minutes. Within five minutes he had lost the rest. He had large animated graphs with detailed diagrams propounding something similar to what the Esperanto group was suggesting. Seemingly endless numbers and abstract concepts surrounded by an aura of esoteric absurdity as its only basic redeeming quality. Most of us thought it was one of the coolest presentations at the conference simply because we couldn't wait to hear what he'd say next. It was so preposterously harebrained that Zhenia, the guy who translated it into English, told me that even the printer refused to print it out for the longest time. Don't get me wrong, the west also has its share of Wacko Jackos, but just different ones.

The reality of routine business protocol also left me aghast. In Sevastopol, Ukraine, I considered buying a television because it was only 766 grevna *(about $140).* "What a deal?" I thought. But after inquiring about it, the salesman quickly clarified things: "Well, that's not really the price."

"Oh really, then what does this 766 grevna mean?" I questioned.

"Oh, well that's last year's price," he replied.

"Okay, well, then what's the current price?" I asked.

"Well, it's presently on sale for 940 grevna," he explained. I asked him why they didn't change the price tag on it and this was his classic response: "Well, we don't want to scare away any customers. I'm sure you understand." Sure I understood, but what I couldn't understand was how the company could imagine that lying to their customers wouldn't terrify them even more. America, frankly, is no stranger to sneaky salesmen either, but the clerk still had me scratching my temple for at least a couple of minutes anyhow. It kind of reminds me of the time when we approached a radio station in Crimea to see how much airtime would cost. The initial answer was $1000 every fifteen seconds. We eventually negotiated a price of $100 an hour on the airwaves but we still decided against it. Another time, in Odessa, someone offered his corroded office space to us for a real bargain according to him, $6000 per month. He informed me that he had been seeking clients for a long time, but still remained confident that some would eventually turn up some day.

"Good luck!" was about all I could tell him. "How do these places stay in business?" I thought. It brought to mind how the majority of Ukrainian restaurants or cafes, back in 1993 at least, would actually close down for lunch only to reopen in the middle of the afternoon when everyone was already back at work. "Doesn't that, like," I deduced, "defeat the purpose?" Rattling as it all was, it did, howbeit, make sense of the following incident.

As I approached the money exchange booth, at Simferopol's train station, a man distracted me by offering me a better exchange rate. Unaware of the law's restrictions and totally green indeed, I chose to play his game. Well, I lost that game along with my crisp new $50 bill. I did, however, get a shiny new $1 bill in the swap. Not exactly the exchange rate I was anticipating. Luckily for me, the man conducting the game had a diamond in one of his two front teeth. Since he was so easy to pinpoint, I assumed that the police might eventually be able to assist me if I filed a complaint. My reception at the police station astounded me, though, as did the expeditious manner in which they operated. "I'd like to report a robbery," I explained.

"No problem!" they answered, all smiling from ear to ear. My conjecture naturally inferred that there would be forms to fill out and at least a short interview, but they promptly bypassed the formalities by posing three brief questions straight away: "Where'd it happen, how much, and what does he look like?" Instantly rejoining my brief responses with sporadic giggles, they chortled: "Oh, yeah, we know that guy. Sure, we'll get your money back for you, but there's one stipulation."

"Ah, what's that?" I asked.

"Invite us all to America one of these days," they joked.

"Ah, sure, no problem!" I muddled.

"Come on!" they chanted, as one cop put a hand on my shoulder and said, "Let's go get him!" After pulling up to the exchange booths in our jeep we immediately noticed that our criminal had fled the scene, however, that didn't matter because the fuzz picked another guy who would do just fine, discounting the fact that I'd never seen him before. He was apparently in cahoots with our fugitive, which didn't bother me. What did bother me was that it was becoming obvious that our fugitive was in cahoots with the police department. After tantalizing him for a few minutes in the jeep, before I knew it I was holding a crisp new $50 bill. "That was simple!" I thought. I actually came out ahead because of the $1 bill I also collected that day. After our prisoner got a rapid release they turned to me to do some rhetorical probing, "Well, what do you think of our police work? Not too shabby, huh?" I was speechless, which happens very seldom. Facilitating a rote understanding of how businesses could blatantly lie to their customers became routine procedure once the police department chose to bare all. Plainly put, this American had lots to learn about this new culture.

Then there was the area of public transport. On March 9, the day after Women's Day in Ukraine, I was returning from the Baptist church in a public minivan and a highly intoxicated female was desperately trying to get into the vehicle but couldn't quite manage. So, I gave her a hand. Well, after nabbing the seat next to me, she proceeded to hit on me throughout the duration of our fifteen-minute ride together. She even clasped onto my hand several times, kissing it passionately. Bystanders couldn't keep from cracking up. The funniest thing was that I had fifty "Jesus Film" posters in my other hand, yet she was the only one who didn't seem to notice. Then there was the boozer on the trolleybus next to me who couldn't stop bumping into me because of the rocky road we were on, and he finally lambasted me too: "Man, would you quit bumping into me already? Get a hold of yourself you dummy!" He was so plastered that he thought I was drunk. Adapting to public transport, like everything else in the former USSR was no stroll in the park either.

On another occasion, I was sitting near two adolescents who noticed that I was a foreigner. After asking me where I was from, I just told them the truth, "New York, originally."

"Oh, come on, you're not from New York!" they argued.

"Ah, yes, I really am!" I affirmed.

"No you're not! Come on, tell us where you're really from!" they pleaded.

"Well, I sincerely cannot understand why it's so hard for you to believe that I'm from New York and whether that be difficult or not, it's still true!" I demanded.

"Look mister, we may be young and all, but we're not naïve! So please stop trying to con us," they insisted, "and give it to us straight already!"

"Well, alright," I conceded, "I guess trying to fool you guys was a big mistake. You got me on that one. I'm really from Congo."

"Congo?" they shouted.

"Yes, Congo!" I yelled back. "Have you heard of it?"

"Of course!" they exclaimed. "They have a great soccer team and since you finally decided to be honest with us we'll be sure to root for them in this year's World Cup," they vowed, "that is, if Ukraine gets eliminated!" By the time we got to the trolleybus stop, we were all but chanting "Congo, Congo, Congo!" repeatedly in the back of the bus. It strained my brain to think that some people more readily accepted my African heritage over my American citizenship, despite the fact that I'm white, redheaded, and Irish.

What was also puzzling was considering how writing with my left hand boggled people's minds. I've been in Ukraine for approximately ten years now and people are still asking me that same question, "Why are you writing with your left hand?" Of course, during Communism, writing with your left hand was highly discouraged, which helps to explain their confusion. Chuck Philips, the missionary to Tatars in Crimea, is also left-handed, and when somebody commented on that fact, he replied, "Why, yes, I'm a bra." Incidentally, the Russian word for "lefty" sounds a lot like the Russian word for "bra" to most Americans. In any case, I think the Communists may have a case, considering how poor my handwriting is. Nevertheless, it still seemed a little weird at first.

The Church also caught me a little off guard here. Following a church service in Ukraine, I once spotted the individuals who had distributed the Lord's Supper pouring the remaining communion wine into a couple of chalices and guzzling it down after a ritualistic toast. In fact, they even did it with big smiles in full view of the whole congregation, during the cleanup process after the service concluded. I instantly emailed my American team with the news, sarcastically remarking: "I desperately wanted to chant, 'Chug, chug, chug!' but I was too busy being in shock."

Chapter Nine
Only in Ukraine!

∽o∾

Several years ago, I was waiting for a trolleybus with my friend, Dima Tunik, and a homeless man approached us. We began talking to him about the Lord and he told us that he was a believer. Now, you must understand that some Protestant groups in Ukraine are in the habit of using those *"Greet one another with a holy kiss" (Romans 16:16, 1 Corinthians 16:20, 2 Corinthians 13:12, 1 Thessalonians 5:26, 1 Peter 5:14)* references very literally. And, apparently, so was this guy. "Since we're all Christians," he proposed, "let's go ahead and greet each other." Well, I thought he was going to hug me until his hug almost landed on my lips. He didn't quite make it but, believe me, it was close enough. Meanwhile, since Dima was out near the street, watching for approaching trolleybuses, he happened to miss that whole exchange. So I quietly told our new friend to lay one on Dima too, whenever he decided to return to us. Being the dedicated friend I was, I wasn't about to leave Dima out of such an unforgettable display of brotherly love. So I made sure to go the extra mile and do the right thing. Well, take my word for it, Dima just about fell over a nearby garbage can trying to avoid that *"holy kiss."* At that, the man turned to me and said, "Wait a second! How can you call yourselves Christians when you act like this?"

"Well," I reasoned, "I know it's hard, but if you can imagine this, we are some of those non-kissing Christians." A homeless drunk, claiming to be a firm believer, yet questioning my faith because I wouldn't kiss him on the lips in public, kind of threw me for a loop if you catch my drift.

Another perplexing scene transpired while watching a popular Hollywood movie on video, in Ukraine, while it was still showing in American movie theaters. Some of my very excited American friends contacted me from the States, urging me to go see it in the movies whenever it got to Ukraine. Their excitement waned a bit when they got wind of my response: "Well, guys, all I can say is that your punctuality leaves a lot to be desired. For your information, not only has the movie already arrived in Ukraine, but I even saw it on video last week. Thanks anyway for the heads up though." Of course, the particular video I saw was the first pirated version of that film to be released there. Most videos and DVD's are pirated there anyway, but the earliest versions are usually of the poorest quality. Hence, rather than getting the impression that I was viewing a multimillion-dollar Hollywood production, I almost felt like I was watching a cheap documentary. The saying "It's much better on the big screen!" would definitely apply here. Anyway, not only was it obviously being taped with a camcorder from the back of the movie theater, due to the fact that people were visibly getting up for snacks or to use the restroom, but it was also the only funny version of this melodrama I've ever had the pleasure of seeing. Even the excruciatingly sad parts were hysterical. For instance, toward the end of this "tear-jerker" there was a very emotional scene where the hero was dying in the arms of his first love. Naturally, she struggled to revive him with passionate cries, repeatedly calling out his name with tears and agony. Yet, despite the dreary picture, it was next to impossible to get emotional because after every one of her impassioned cries came the monotone voice of the Russian translator, needlessly repeating the hero's name. On top of that, either the man taping the film or the guy next to him, unable to control his grief, burst out sobbing right into the camera's microphone. Thus, one of history's saddest films became one of the best comedies of the year. Hence, Ukraine, once again, retained its reputation as the land where almost nothing ever made sense.

Even Ukraine's insect world left lasting impressions on me. Aside from the roaches and mosquitoes in Kiev, Ukraine introduced me to some of the most bizarre flies I've ever encountered. On one occasion, I was reading in my room when the Abominable Fly started buzzing around feverishly. After what seemed like an eternity of non-stop buzzing noise, there was a break in the action that just filled the room with a heavenly silence. I was overjoyed to have spotted him lying flat on his back, directly under my reading lamp on the desk. My guess was that he had received his just punishment by flying straight into the lamp and absorbing a few jolts and volts. Assuming he was out of my life forever, I blew on him in hopes of giving him a proper burial behind my desk. However, he immediately awakened from his slumber and resumed his obnoxious noise making. It was crazy! I'd never seen anything like it before. To my knowledge, American flies aren't in the habit of lying on their backs directly under lamps for either relaxation or tanning purposes, but we were clearly a long way from the USA.

On another occasion, I was spending the night with some Tatar friends whose house was regularly replete with various buzzing things, the majority of which were probably flies in one form or another *(though I can't verify that for sure)*. Given the fact that there was no electricity in the village, and because it was late at night, we could hear them much better than we could actually see them. Since I couldn't believe my ears, I wanted my eyes to confirm what I was hearing. So I lit a match. Well, the fly population in that room was so enormous that one actually flew into the flame itself, burning off its wing. Our main entertainment for the next few minutes was watching him hop around till we ran out of matches. They say that there are three signs of middle age. The first is losing one's memory but I can't remember the other two. In any respect, whether I'm approaching middle age or not, for the life of me I cannot remember anything remotely like that ever happening in America. "Only in Ukraine," as the say.

"Alright, all the talk about this 'strange country' is understandable," you say, "but why were they so confused about you?" Well, that's another story altogether. Two key reasons justify their bewilderment: 1) I was an American, and 2) I was a dumb American. For example, I once ventured out in search of some decent shaving cream, but I was unfamiliar with the European brands being sold. So I attempted to sniff them all until I found one whose scent was undetectable. Captivated and rather determined, I practically put the nozzle inside my nose as I accidentally applied excessive force to the valve. Well, within milliseconds, I had gobs of shaving cream in my nose. "Ah, I don't want that one," I huffed, just before my notorious disappearing act. If you're not convinced yet, well, don't fret because there's much more.

In 1995, as a full-time missionary in Kharkov, Ukraine, I was conducting a series of lectures on evidence for the resurrection of Christ through my interpreter Vika. We had thoroughly discussed some pretty pertinent points along the way, but there was still one fact that I wanted them to come up with on their own. I kept probing and hinting at the idea, but they still couldn't figure out what I was getting at. Finally, Vika's mother, a former Communist who was visiting our lectures for the first time figured that she had the answer: "John, don't worry because I know what you're trying to say." Turning to the group assembled there she promptly explained, "Friends, John is merely emphasizing that we're not even sure that Jesus ever even existed at all." Nodding at me, she asked, "Am I right?"

"Well, that's certainly an interesting idea," I muttered, "but not quite what I was looking for. Thanks anyway." Calling on the wrong person at the right time is a great way to shoot yourself in the foot, which happens to be one of my favorite pastimes. Another time, while delivering a speech at a symposium in Yalta, Ukraine, just before attempting to make an important point, I asserted, "From this evidence we can all see...well, alright, most of us can see...okay, well, at least I can see." At that point, another American presenting a paper there, Bill Altman, burst out laughing. While that may have added a little humor to the conference, it certainly didn't do much for the point I intended to make.

A Dumb American in a Strange Country

Even when I was a child, I'd always don this facetious smirk whenever I got in trouble. After getting caught with my hand in the cookie jar, that smirk would just surface like clockwork, even though that was the last thing on earth that I wanted to do. It was just a nervous smile that I couldn't get rid of no matter how hard I tried, which thoroughly irked my parents for the longest time. There were usually very painful consequences as a result of it too, that is, until one day when my father very calmly warned me, "John, I'm telling you for the last time, wipe that smirk off your face or I'm going to do it for you."

Finally, after the tears started streaming down my cheeks, I cried, "Dad, you've got to believe me, I don't want to smile, but I can't help it! I DON'T WANT TO SMILE!" At last, my parents understood that it was simply a nervous smile rather than a conniving one. Life certainly got much easier after clearing that up. However, drawing negative attention to myself became a hard habit to break. In fact, I'm still working on it.

I also performed that vanishing act on the trolleybus once or twice. I was standing near the center door, waiting for it to open so I could get out. The problem was that we were just pulling up to a red traffic light, directly adjacent to the bus stop. Whenever the light is red, at that particular stop in Crimea, many drivers just let their passengers off at the light because of how close it is to the actual bus stop itself. And that's exactly what I was betting on this time. But as I gently lifted my right foot, while holding onto the pole to my right, expecting the door to swing open, the driver put the "pedal to the metal" for about two seconds. Two seconds was more than enough in a situation like that one. The next thing I knew, I was not only lying on my back, but I was also in some poor lady's lap. It wasn't just any ordinary lady either. It happened to be an indignant one holding a dozen eggs in an open container. So, coupled with the egg on my face, I had eggs all over my back and in my hair too. In addition to the woman yelling obscenities and probably getting ready to dump the rest of the eggs on my head, I quickly spotted two open trolleybus doors and made yet another grand leaping exit, this time, fortunately with no cops in sight.

85

That was almost as embarrassing as the time when I was teaching at Crimean-American College in Sevastopol, Ukraine. I had been lecturing for about an hour before we decided to take a short break. But during the break, one of the students took me out into the hallway and told me that my zipper was down, which, admittedly was probably some of the most beneficial information conveyed during that whole semester. And as wacky as it may sound, that was a mere warm up for what happened next.

Chapter Ten
Learning to laugh . . . at yourself

After being forced out of Dubke and into Simferopol proper, I lived with a Russian family for about seven months. It was then that I met Nicolai and Luda Gluhi, who would later become my host family. Nicolai was a baseball coach who was used to raising his voice on the baseball diamond, so he would sometimes do that with me on the phone since my Russian was so poor then. Repeating to me the same Russian phrases verbatim was common because many people assumed that if they'd repeat the same exact words, only louder, then perhaps I'd finally understand. Apparently many thought I had a problem with my hearing instead of my Russian. I remember hanging up the phone after a conversation with Nicolai and telling Lena, my hostess, "Gee, that man always yells on the phone and I can't figure out why."

"Maybe he's *gluhoi*," Lena suggested.

"What's *gluhoi*?" I asked.

"The word *'gluhoi'* means 'deaf' in Russian," Lena explained.

"Yeah, that's a pretty strong possibility," I quipped, "since Nicolai's last name is Gluhi." *(Gluhi is actually the plural form of gluhoi.)*

Anyway, Nicolai asked me if I would play on their baseball team for a few games. Perhaps I was in a crazy-zany-giddy-up mood when I acquiesced in spite of my eleven-year layoff, but I couldn't play until I made my little visit to the clinic. A physical was required for every player. While nervously standing in front of a whole panel of female nurses, one of them issued the order: *"Rozdevaiyca!"* Well, there are varying definitions for that Russian word, two of which are, "Take your coat off and stay a while," or "take your clothes off." All of the nurses immediately began discussing something amongst themselves, but I still attempted to get her attention with a brief question.

"Ah, completely?" I squealed.

Overly preoccupied with her colleagues, and unaware of my confusion, she quickly turned to me and said, "Come on, what are you waiting for? Get on with it already!" I glanced at Nicolai, playfully requesting that he do an about-face.

With a chuckle he said, "Be a good boy and do what the doctor says."

Well, when my shorts hit the floor and all the nurses started gawking instead of talking, the head nurse finally grasped the severity of the situation, yelling, "Just your shirt! Just your shirt!" Well, in my view, it was just a little too late for explanations because the damage was already done. After the examination, she asked if I was a professional or an amateur, but I wisely chose to let Nicolai handle that question.

Still not convinced that I'm a dumb American in a strange country? In my first year as a full-time missionary, I lived in Kharkov, Ukraine. I not only approached a Russian woman saying, "Good duck," instead of "Good morning," but I also wound up asking my hostess if she had a child out of wedlock *(zachala)* rather than asking her if she noticed something *(zamichala)*. The fact that my friend Nathan told his Bible study group, "I have heaven in my shower," instead of saying, "I have heaven in my soul," didn't make me feel much better either. On the other hand, the fact that he told our Ukrainian minister that he liked "hot and spicy Georgian fornication" *(blude)* instead of "hot and spicy Georgian cuisine" *(bluda)* did help some, though I was just getting warmed up myself.

A Dumb American in a Strange Country

In the middle of my sermon, during my first year as a full-time missionary, despite the fact that I was using a translator, I still attempted to say one line in my broken Russian. It was freezing cold outside and we were without heat in our facility that day. So I tried to look on the bright side: "At least you won't fall asleep during my sermon today." Unfortunately, what I actually said sounded more like: "At least you won't contract AIDS during my sermon." Granted, that is a valid point if you really think about it. And you can rest assured that nobody fell asleep during that message. Additionally, I accidentally informed my friend that it was after my "circumcision" *(obrezania)* that I came to Ukraine, instead of saying that it was following my "education" *(obrazivania)* that I did so. While that may have been accurate, it was a bit more transparent than I planned on being. It was almost as bad as the time I referred to "the burps *(otrishki)* of Scripture," instead of "the passages *(otrivki)* of Scripture."

In all honesty, Russian wasn't the only language that temporarily ruined my reputation. At a particular Tatar home, the host was so drunk that he just couldn't get the hint that we wanted out of there no matter what we did. He would, at times, break out into spontaneous laughter and then, before you knew it, he was sobbing like a baby. At least he remained very consistent with his redundant official Arabic greeting that we heard every five minutes, "Asalom Aleykum."

I was also rather consistent with the proper reply, "Aleykum Asalom," that is until one careless slip of my American tongue that almost sobered him up: "Saleykom alom." Of course, there isn't a foreigner alive who hasn't told a Russian that he urinated *(peesil)* on a piece of paper instead of writing *(peesol)* on it. In fact, I still stumble on that one at times. Oddly enough, the superabundance of language blunders added to my level of popularity in this strange new place but that certainly didn't help my IQ any.

Strangely though, I decided not to stop there either. I once tried calling my friend Miriam, immediately shouting, "Hey baldilla!" *('Hey stupid!')* into the phone. I reckoned that it was her on the other end, but I reckoned wrong. After the lady sternly asked who I was seeking, several times, I realized that Miriam was both somewhere and someone else. Hanging up very gently without a word seemed to be my only viable recourse. Although contacting Miriam would have been considered fairly urgent, I preferred calling her back another day.

All extroverts habitually think out loud, that is, except for the dumb ones. The dumb ones tend to do just the opposite; they *don't think* out loud! That was definitely me after my arrival. That's like when I requested heaping mounds of extra mustard on my hotdog, totally unaware that it was Russian mustard. The generic container threw me off completely. For the curious out there, Russian mustard is *a lot hotter* than American brands. It's not for the faint of heart! With tears flowing and my nose running profusely I revisited the lady saying, "Wow, this is one great hotdog. *And boy is it hot too!*"

Not thinking out loud can be dangerous! *(So don't try this at home.)* My friend, Shariya, can certainly vouch for that. Shariya is an elderly Tatar woman who had been feeling a bit under the weather. What made things worse was that she was unlucky enough to run into me, in my own neighborhood, which is basically as far away from her apartment as one could go in that city. Shariya described how she was feeling so I instinctively invited her to my place for some hot tea, hoping that would help some. When my host family got home they asked me, "Who'd you make tea for?"

"Shariya," I answered. Well, after laughing almost to the point of dry heaving, they informed me that the tea was a special mixture of tea and laxatives due to some problems a family member had been having. Luckily, it was a special laxative with a delayed reaction of at least several hours, allowing Shariya to finish her errands and get home safely. However, checking on Shariya the following day as you've surely guessed, was at the top of my priority list.

"Well, my headache is definitely gone," she explained, "but this morning, while I was on the phone, I had this insatiable urge to make a mad dash to the commode and almost didn't make it in time. I tossed the phone receiver and had to call my friend back to apologize. I'm not exactly sure what's going on with my stomach right now but I am sure that it can't be very good!" At that point, my conscience was using its megaphone: "Should I tell her the truth or just let it go?" Naturally, I let it go. But the cat's surely out of the bag now.

A Dumb American in a Strange Country

Ruslan was an eleven-year old Tatar boy with whom I lived in Dubke. We were all scheduled to go on a field trip together, accompanying his classmates to a children's theater. Waiting for the rest of the students on one of the many bus stops at the convolutedly befogging Central Market, in Simferopol, the few of us present realized that we were all going to be late.

"They might be waiting for us at one of the other stops here," one boy concluded. "Maybe we ought to start looking for them." Somebody quickly read all of our minds, commenting about the choice to meet in such a confusing place like the Central Market.

Again, with the extrovert getting the best of me, I opened my big fat mouth, "Who is the moron that arranged for us to meet at the Central Market, of all places?"

Giggling with glee, "Our school teacher," somebody tittered.

Well, before we wrap this up, let's just put a little icing on the cake to eliminate any doubts about how much of an extroverted American I really was. I met a wonderful Tatar family a few years ago. In fact, it was at Marcel's home where the fly burnt his wing off, if that rings a bell. Anyway, the first time I approached their house to visit them, their giant dog met me in the yard, showing nothing but yellow teeth. And he had lots of them. But he was pretty old and his bite wasn't nearly as fierce as that puny little mutt who received two boots in the jaw before my first visit at another Tatar home. That actually occurred in full view of the hostess, by the way. What a way to kick off a relationship, right? Anyway, their dog tried to show that it still had some bite left in him. Luckily, Marcel's sons rescued me in the knick of time without any bloodshed. Well, before the close of my first visit with Marcel's family, he reiterated the fact that I was always welcome and that whenever the dog chose to present any resistance that I should just shout, "Ayisha," which would supposedly forestall and even prevent any potential tragedies along the way.

During my second visit, though, when the family brought up something about their old dog, I hastily replied, "Oh, you mean Ayisha?"

"No, no," they retorted. "Ayisha is our mother!" Starting relationships off well is probably not one of my talents, especially when vicious canines enter the picture.

"Well, John," you're probably wondering, "what exactly are you getting at here?" It's actually pretty simple. Life has PLANETARY POTENTIAL for being a bona fide adventure, especially when you step out of your comfort zone for His sake. Who needs the mundane when the center of His will can offer us so much more? The truth is that I never would have ended up in this strange new discovery zone were it not for Him. Were it not for His perfect plan, I never would have experienced the extremities of life, maximizing all the good and bad that another culture can offer us. Jesus, in John 10:10, promises His true followers *"life... to the full."* In my case, He definitely delivered. You see, no matter how all of my experiences might sound to you, I wouldn't trade them for the world because of all the wonderful memories I'll take with me and because of all that I've learned in the process. "How does that relate to me?" you ask. Well, if God can work in and through me, a dumb American in a strange country, whose heart was merely halfway open most of the time, then He can certainly do the same with you. If you ever find yourself in a strange place or circumstance for Jesus' sake, then just remember that He usually has a unique way of teaching you to lighten up and laugh at yourself in some very healthy ways. After all, in strange places, especially, you have no other option but to laugh at yourself because everyone else already is. And, as odd as it may sound, that maturing process usually tends to be both immeasurably satisfying and loads of fun too. And, who knows, maybe you, too, will end up with a few stories for the rest of us.

Part Three:
Some God-lessons for the Road!

Chapter Eleven
Finding God's will isn't entirely doing God's will!

∽○∾

*T*he *following are some guidelines from the American Food and Drug Administration:*

❖ Apple Butter – if the mold count is 12% or more, or if it averages four rodent hairs for every 100 grams, or if it averages five or more whole insects per 100 grams, the FDA will pull it from the shelves. *(Otherwise, it goes right onto your bagels.)*

❖ Mushrooms – they can't be sold if there's an average of twenty or more maggots of any size per 15 grams of dried mushrooms. *(Otherwise, bon appetite.)*

❖ Fig Paste – if there are more than 13 insect heads per 100 grams in each of two or more sub-samples, the whole batch is tossed. *(What a relief, huh?)*

❖ Hot Dogs – YOU DON'T WANT TO KNOW! *(Thank goodness for the FDA.)*

Anyway, the point is that it's hard to find pure anything these days. Even 50% of bottled water is contaminated. But that's especially the case when we're talking about moral issues. Try finding complete honesty these days. A toddler Sunday school teacher asked her class, "Why is it necessary to be quiet in church?" "Because people are sleeping," one bright little girl replied.

Unfortunately, toddlers seem to have a monopoly on honesty nowadays. Complete joy is just as rare, but the Bible offers some very practical answers here. In 1992, I saw a play about Jesus in Cincinnati. It stunk! The play depicted Jesus as a man who experienced absolutely no joy whatsoever. He couldn't even crack a smile. Don't you think that Jesus felt joy when Peter called Him the *"Christ"* for the first time ever? Don't you think Jesus felt joy when Lazarus came forth from the tomb? Don't you think He was jubilant when the Samaritan woman brought back half her town to hear the truth? According to the original Greek, in Hebrews 12:2, Jesus even viewed the cross with a sense of joy. But how did He do it?

Luke 10:17-21 indicates that Jesus experienced unspeakable joy because God's will was getting accomplished. The fulfillment of His Father's will automatically produced that emotion within Jesus' life. I think that's pretty important because it's one of many Biblical examples showing how joy is inevitably linked with doing God's will. In John 15, Jesus tells His disciples that He is the Vine and they, like us, are the branches. So we're not just intimately linked with Him, but He is our only real source of life. In John 15:10-11, Jesus tells them to obey Him: *"If you obey my commands, you will remain in my love, just as I have obeyed my Father's commands and remain in His love. I have told you this so that my joy may be in you and that your joy may be complete."* You see, Jesus gives us His joy when we obey Him, and when we obey Him with the right attitudes and motives, our natural joy gets mixed in with His supernatural joy to make our joy perfect or complete. See, the key to experiencing complete joy is broken up into two parts: 1) doing God's will so that God can give us His joy, and 2) joyfully doing God's will with pure motives. Then, and only then, can we experience complete joy.

Some folks, of course, present divergent views on how to obtain joy. In Buddhism, for example, the way to obtain joy is by eliminating all of your desires altogether. The problem is that the system doesn't work because you must first have the desire to do so. Some feel that worry is the great killjoy in the universe. Hence, getting rid of worry is the key. When Francis Schaeffer would converse with people who'd confidently say that they'd finally found complete joy in life by successfully eliminating every last worry, he'd usually burst their bubble by saying, "Ah, excuse me, but, I think you're in DIRE NEED OF A TIC TAC!" As always, their arrogant smiles instantaneously mutated into flustered blushes. Why? Simply because they still tend to worry about what others think. And, regardless of what they might say, that'll always be the case. It's like the humanist who says that there are no moral absolutes out there. Yeah, well try taking his briefcase and see what he says then.

Some of you may remember John Cage, who claimed that joy came from the cosmos by chance. He was a musician who wrote *"music"* based solely upon hundreds of coin tosses, expressing his theory of chance. During his concerts, however, he would also get booed off stage, oftentimes by his own musicians. So, while theories may abound, I submit that real joy, rather than coming from somewhere, actually comes from Someone. Still, let's be mindful of the fact that that Someone has set conditions for receiving it.

At the dedication of the wall in Jerusalem, during the time of the prophet Nehemiah, there was great joy. Nehemiah 12:43 reads: *"And on that day they offered great sacrifices, rejoicing because God had given them great joy... The sound of rejoicing in Jerusalem could be heard far away."* Here, we see that it was God who gave the people great joy. The question is why. One reason is because the people finished the wall, which was God's will. The other reason is because of the manner in which they did it. Nehemiah 4:6 not only explains how the people poured their hearts into the work, but verses eight and nine show that in order to fight opposition against their building efforts, before strapping on any worldly weapons, the people immediately decided to trust God with their divine weapon of prayer. Nehemiah 5:14-16 even confirms that the prophet himself, instead of abusing his privileges as the new head honcho in charge, gladly chose to do God's work God's way. And the result was abundant joy.

Joy often eludes us, though, because doing God's will isn't always easy. The Israelites had their opposition and we have ours. While ministering at Willow Creek Community Church, John Ortberg wrote an excellent book called: *The Life You Always Wanted*. The following is a short excerpt:

> "The ministry of bearing with one another is more than simply tolerating difficult people. It is also learning to hear God speak through them. It is learning to be for them. It is learning that the difficult person I have most to deal with is me. This means that a part of the ministry to which I am called is to free people – repeatedly if necessary – from the little mental prisons to which I consign them. It may be a person who criticizes the way I teach, whether justly, or unjustly, lovingly or spitefully. It may be the most difficult person of all – one in whom I see the same struggles that rage inside me. Bearing with them does not require becoming best friends, but means learning to wish them well, releasing our right to hurt them back, coming to experience our common standing before the cross" *(1997, p. 117)*.

Wow, now that's tough! But, unless you and I can actually do that, we'll never completely reach the center of God's will. We'll neither be able to accomplish with His might what He has planned for us, nor will we ever develop the attitude that will permit complete joy to invade our very lives. See, it's the person who has chosen not to forgive; it's the person who has decided that the grudge is sovereign; it's the person whose own will gets top priority; it's that kind of person who usually achieves merely some counterfeited-sugar-coated version of fleeting happiness and success, frequently ending up miserable in the end rather than obtaining perfect joy that endures in all circumstances.

Just ask Ted Turner, who dreamt of becoming a billionaire all his life. Finally, when his life-long goal became a reality, he excitedly sped home to tell his wife the news. In record time, though, he was forced to swallow a God-lesson on the spot. "Honey," he shouted, "I've got the best news in the world for you today! We're billionaires!"

"Great! Wonderful!" she sarcastically retorted. "Now, if you've got a few minutes to spare, take a coffee break and help your kids with their homework!"

"What a disappointment!" Turner confessed in a subsequent interview. *That's because perfect joy is a gift from God (Galatians 5:22)*, only to be fully experienced in His presence, in His will, and in His way. The New Testament simply calls this: *"living by the Spirit."*

Early on, I was not sure what I wanted to do with my life. At first, I wanted to become a professional baseball player until I realized that I couldn't even chew gum and tie my cleats simultaneously, much less chew tobacco and play in the major leagues. Then, I set my sights on being a bodybuilder until I realized that I didn't have the body for it. Later on, I considered some other options, probably more out of necessity. Thankfully, by the time I hit seventeen my thinking became a bit more rational, meaning that Christian ministry was about all I could see myself doing. On the other side of the coin, that didn't mean that there weren't any major detours. Allow me to elaborate.

In 1994, I spent my first year as a full-time missionary in Kharkov, Ukraine, facilitating a church plant. Within two weeks after our arrival on the scene, we baptized sixteen people into Christ, following a three-day festival attended by approximately 1,400 people each evening. By approximately our five-month marker, aside from my work with our growing congregation, I was also a weekly guest Bible lecturer in two public schools, as well as at Kharkov's prestigious university. Moreover, I was conducting two Bible studies consisting predominantly of English speaking students and alumni interpreters, eventually forming the nucleus for a thriving campus ministry. Withal, adding to our growing church attendance, which hit at least 100 inside the first year, I gladly immersed six individuals through my own personal evangelistic efforts. In fact, one of them was somebody I happened to have met on the bus. We struck up a quick conversation about Jesus Christ that lasted about five bus-stops long. On the sixth, he and I got out of the bus and I subsequently baptized him in the river. He even joined our congregation and served faithfully from that point on. "Hey, this is productivity!" I thought. Sadly, the bigger our church got, the bigger my head got. That's right, I was too busy patting myself on the back to notice God tapping me on the shoulder.

Here we were back at square one again. When God gave me the desires of my heart, instead of fully relinquishing it to Him, like I should have done, I basically said, "Hey, God, thanks a lot for the great suggestions. I'm sure they'll come in handy once in a while." Selfishly taking God's advice, no matter what that might mean, without reciprocating on His terms, isn't quite the way He's designed it all to work. That's selfishly squandering His blessings; that's poor stewardship. And, whether I realized it or not, that's what I was doing. See, finding God's plan doesn't mean you've arrived; it just means that you finally know what road to take. My mistake wasn't taking the wrong road; it was hopping into the driver's seat instead of handing Him the keys. My mistake was failing to utterly depend on God by truly *"living by the Spirit."* As a result, despite all of the productivity during that first year, my spiritual life was in shambles. In fact, I ended up further away from the Lord than when I initially began. And that just goes to show that the relinquishing of our hearts to God is only the first step in a lengthy process. Stepping into God's backyard is an essential first step. That's all! Deciding to write a book and actually holding a published copy in your hands are two entirely different things. Likewise, finally choosing God's path instead of your own is still a far cry from Romans 8:13-14, Romans 12:1-3, Ephesians 5:1, Philippians 2:13, and 1 John 3:9. A little later, we'll discuss how God turned the tables on my circumstances in order to teach me a similar lesson.

Chapter Twelve
God's plan and my personality

S olomon wrote, *"Pride goes before destruction, a haughty spirit before a fall" (Proverbs 16:18).* Without divulging all the juicy details, let's just say that I was living proof of that statement because my pride turned me into the kind of person I never thought I'd become. While I was able to finally acknowledge that fact, I still failed to see that God was trying desperately to get my attention. I guess that just emphasizes the extent of my detachment and self-absorption. Nonetheless, after taking several months in America to get my head deflated and screwed back on right, Solomon's words in Proverbs 11:2 made more sense: *"When pride comes, then comes disgrace, but with humility comes wisdom."* God, by subsequently sending me to work with Crimean Tatars, near the Black Sea, had only begun to force-feed me the true meaning of those words. It would be yet another two years before I began gaining the type of humility needed for recognizing that simple kind of godly wisdom I had lacked all my life. Even then, the mandatory process of embracing my foolishness in order to increase my spiritual savvy *(see 1 Corinthians 3:18)*, shamefully seemed rather involuntary.

Dick Alexander, a minister in Ohio, visited with a personal friend of mine, who is also an excellent translator from Kherson

Christian Church in Ukraine. "Vlad," Alexander asked, "is there anything specific about Ukraine that we Americans should be praying about?"

"I'm uncomfortable when Americans ask that question," Vlad remarked, "because they usually want to pray about our economy. Had our economy not been so poor, our new church would never have been born. Had that been the case, I wouldn't be a Christian today. So, please don't pray that our lives would be easy. Pray, rather, that we would be strong." Truthfully, my faith didn't even compare with Vlad's, and sometimes I doubt that it ever will.

Vlad's selfless no-strings-attached faith both honors God and embodies the core of wisdom's essence. That kind of faith, common to active believers in the former USSR, permanently established Ukraine's reputation, in my American mind, as a "Strange Country." "Knowledge is power!" America whoops, acting like that is the heart of wisdom. Some claim that relevance is the path to wisdom. Others contend that anything is wisdom as long as it brings results. There may be grains of truth in all of the available theories, but I submit that a humble and sacrificial faith is the real key to wisdom. Solomon was a fairly wise man in his own right, and the context of his famous words, *"The fear of the Lord is the beginning of knowledge, but fools... despise discipline" (Proverbs 1:7)*, implies that wisdom is actually a powerful yearning to know God, not information. James also prudently advises: *"Who is wise and understanding among you? Let him show it by his good life, by deeds done in the humility that comes from wisdom... For where you have envy and selfish ambition, there you find disorder and every evil practice. But the wisdom that comes from heaven is first of all pure; then peace loving, considerate, submissive, full of mercy and good fruit, impartial and sincere" (James 3:13, 16-17)*. Genuine wisdom, like real joy, is a gift that is only available at God's kiosk, as Vlad would surely concur. And His kiosk is always open 24/7, as long as we are not using the devil's money.

By now you would have thought that I was wise enough to learn my lesson. I wasn't. Oh, I was well aware of my life's messy details, but apparently I still needed a few more God-lessons before getting the point. Perhaps you can relate. Some God-lessons are like chapters, others are like books, and then there are the ones like diplomas, the latter usually just showing us how dumb we really are, like I mentioned before. Sure, we're all spiritual rocket-scientists in retrospect, but we still have to face the future by living in the present, which sometimes forces even those diploma-like-lessons to the back of our memory banks. Even Kharkov's diploma, which began in the "I'll-never-forget-that-no-matter-how-long-I-live-category," gradually became a distant memory as did the following God-lesson. Nevertheless, the good news is that they both still made it into this book, extending forth a tiny ray of hope for this seemingly senile American redhead.

Kharkov was quite a lesson, but it only had the impact of a Scud Missile because the root of my congenital pride condition remained under the surface. It was a stronghold that still needed some attention. Oh, I knew about the pride, but my pride didn't allow me to take it as seriously as I ought to have. While changing my surroundings might have been a solution, it was only a temporary one. At that point, I was like a half-witted version of Solomon, who swimmingly squandered the majority of his God-lessons because of his arrogance. After Solomon built the temple, a privilege the Lord deprived dear old Dad of, God appeared to him in 1 Kings 9: *"If you walk before me in integrity of heart and uprightness, as David your father did...I will establish your royal throne over Israel forever" (vv. 4-5)*. In the next chapter, after getting some pretty hefty compliments from the Queen of Sheba, we see these words about the king: *"King Solomon was greater in riches and wisdom than all the other kings of the earth. The whole world sought audience with Solomon to hear the wisdom God had put in his heart" (1 Kings 10:23-24)*. Just six verses later, we see how Solomon's pride brought him spiritually lower than he'd ever been before. By the end of chapter eleven, Solomon is forced to file chapter eleven in just about every sense of the word. In fact, after God, through the prophet Ahijah, told Solomon's successor that He would *"humble David's descendants" (1 Kings 11:39)*, Solomon's life and reign abruptly ends. Now, I was no wise king by any stretch of the imagination but I did have a subtly recurring pride problem and, as in Solomon's case, God was watching.

Incidentally, our Esperanto friends were actually onto something because spiritual growth is a lot like math; either you get it or you don't. If you have all of the ingredients except one, you'll never solve the issues at hand. From Christ's words to the Pharisees, *"I desire mercy, not sacrifice" (Matthew 9:13)*, it's clear that they missed the Messiah even when He was speaking to them on the street corner because they followed God with their rituals instead of their hearts. Paul wrote: *"If I have a faith that can move mountains, but have not love, I am nothing. If I give all I possess to the poor and surrender my body to the flames, but have not love, I gain nothing" (1 Corinthians 13:2-3)*.

Several years back, on the mission field, there were some very difficult issues that I had been dealing with. What made things worse was the fact that I began skipping my daily quiet time with the Lord. I basically tried to confront those issues alone, which didn't work very well. And, during that time, God taught me a lesson that I'll never forget. For years I had studied the Bible for the wrong reasons. Much of the time it was for the sake of information. Yes, it was in-depth study, but it was shallow because my motives were shallow. This time, however, it was different because I had gotten to a point in my life where I had to either close up shop, spiritually speaking, or make a radical change. For the first time in my life, I began picking up my Bible daily because I couldn't live without it. I began reading its passages, the Psalms especially, because I desperately needed them. After all those years of studying, for the first time in my life, I finally began to understand how powerfully alive it really is. For the first time in my life it was all finally starting to make sense. And I was so thankful that my life began to change, gradually enabling me to handle those problems with some serenity. I wasn't just reading the Bible anymore; I was worshiping through Scripture and I could say with Jeremiah, *"When your words came, I ate them; they were my joy and my heart's delight" (Jeremiah 15:16)*.

Learning to worship through Bible study was a vital step forward in my quest for freedom from the spiritual prison I had erected. Seminary had taught me about the doctrine of God's heart and my summer internship showed me how far I had strayed from it, but it was the outworking of my iniquities that always seemed to direct my clumsy baby-steps in the right direction for finding it. From Kharkov I was scheduled to head due south to the Crimean Peninsula where additional higher learning was inevitable. My task was to minister to Tatars, the Muslim people group I had met on my summer internship. Yet, in spite of my overconfidence issues, I was still feeling rather overwhelmed to say the least. I knew what needed to be done but felt somewhat helpless because I didn't have the slightest inkling on how to go about doing it. The fact that I was beginning a pioneer work, all by myself, just added to my lonely anxiety levels. Fortunately, that's exactly what I needed because it allowed God to function by keeping my arrogance at bay. God, howbeit, didn't halt His plan for Crimea on account of my own spiritual instability. Nope. He decided to actively promote both of those projects simultaneously. Of course, overseeing the efforts of a brainless missionary with narcissistic leanings is a job only He's capable of handling adequately.

Chapter Thirteen
Doubts, concerns, and answers

⚮

During my humbling debriefing in America, just before moving to Crimea, I was attempting to devise an outreach plan for the Tatars. Well, that may have been the most humiliating facet of my transition phase because I remained clueless even after six months of prayer and reflexive brainstorming. I started feeling like I was back on that bus to Dubke all over again. Helplessly disillusioned, doubt-ridden enough to begin questioning my motives for returning, brain-baffled and frustrated, scared out of my wits, and all alone in my brand new world of self-abasement doesn't even begin to describe my emotional makeup at that stage. But, as the apostle Paul would avow in 2 Corinthians 12:9-10, unbeknownst to me, I was squarely on my way toward God's intended destination for my life. My indigenous sense of pride, back on its heels for a change, blinded me to that reality because although my Kharkov diploma temporarily knocked me down a notch or two, granted, it didn't turn me into a humble person. All joking aside, Moses expressed a peerlessly unassuming attitude by openly admitting the following about himself: *"Moses was . . . more humble than anyone else on the face of the earth" (Numbers 12:3).* Still, the Lord had lots to teach him at that point. Today, I still can't even begin to consciously admit possessing any substantial amount of humility and that frightens me because it means that God's school for me is not only in session but might also continue throughout all eternity. Let's just say that in addition to being a dumb American, I'm also a slow learner.

The prophet Isaiah records God's words to the Jews in chapter 57: *"I live in a high and holy place, but also with him who is contrite and lowly in spirit, to revive the spirit of the lowly and revive the heart of the contrite. I will not accuse forever, nor will I always be angry, for then the spirit of man would grow faint before me- - the breath of man that I have created" (vv.15-16).* The Lord explains the Jews' problem in the following chapter. The fact is that they had no intention of changing within because they were satisfied with who they already were. All they did was try to take the easy way out by strapping a flimsy little Band-Aid on the core issue in the form of a few prayers and a quick fast. God continued in Isaiah 58:4-5: *"You cannot fast as you do today and expect your voice to be heard on high. Is this the kind of fast I have chosen, only a day for a man to humble himself? Is it only for bowing one's head like a reed and for lying on sackcloth and ashes? Is that what you call a fast, a day acceptable to the Lord?"* Their quick fast was supposedly a quick fix, but God usually doesn't operate that way. The chapter goes on to describe true fasting as a true change of heart, attitude, and behavior, which tends to be a lifelong endeavor. It's appalling to contemplate how the Jews deliberately misunderstood God's expectation of interior renovation to accompany exterior liturgy even after He redundantly belabored that point. Again, we see that the state of the heart influences the condition of the eyes and ears. It's also embarrassing to acknowledge that I was in the same boat because my six-month furlough was nothing but an exterior bandage for my internal bleeding. However, it wouldn't be long before the Great Physician intervened.

It was early December, 1995, and in just two weeks I'd be flying off to Crimea. My immediate family would no longer be there for me. All my security blankets were going up in smoke. And my emotions were so acutely wired that I probably could have enrolled at any school of art on the planet without any talent whatsoever. I was practically approaching the microphone with cottonmouth and nothing to say. Overall, not a very good feeling no matter how much I needed it. I had a similar feeling, a few years ago, while sleeping on the top bunk in a cold Ukrainian train. I woke up in the middle of the night and, almost before I could open my eyes, I realized I was already sitting upright because my tummy was telling me something fowl. Well, about the time I got the message, so did the lady on the bottom bunk because she got a rude awakening to say the least. I vomited three times within fifteen seconds, which might actually be a new Ukrainian-train record, creating three new enemies for me in the process. Tossing me out of their compartment for the rest of the night was a unanimous decision *(I obviously didn't get to vote)*. And my apology, the next morning, didn't carry much weight as you could imagine. Likewise, with only two weeks left before my departure, my nerves were making me overly nauseous and Tums wasn't going to spell relief this time. So what did I do? I checked my email.

I got an email from a guy named Jerry Perkins. I'd never heard of this man before nor did I have the slightest hint as to how he had acquired my email address. Coincidentally, he happened to be a missionary in Yalta, Ukraine, which is about two hours from where I would be living in Crimea. He was running Youth With A Mission's *(YWAM's)* training camp for anyone interested in working with Crimean Tatars. Well, that was news to me because I didn't even know that anything like that existed. In his note, he introduced himself and mentioned that he had an American team that was scheduled to arrive in early January *(just after my arrival on the scene)* for some training, and then they would be looking for temporary ministry opportunities as a sort of hands-on continuation of their educational agenda. So Jerry threw that out to me, wondering if I could show them the ropes and use their help for a couple of weeks.

"Well, Jerry," I replied, "I'm completely incompetent in this area since I have almost no experience, myself, but if you send them my way I'll work with them." Amazingly, combining a clueless missionary with a clueless team turned out to be the perfect plan because, within those two weeks, we were able to put our heads together and come up with a powerful working strategy for my pioneer ministry. So the ministry got off the ground with some clear direction and we never looked back. Well, maybe I shouldn't say "never" because there were lots of subsequent concerns that caused me all kinds of grief, as will soon be obvious.

In any case, Jerry sent me other international teams, including a Russian/Ukrainian team as well as a Danish group. That allowed me to immediately step into a leadership role and make some friendships at a time when I needed them most, since almost all of the American missionaries in the city had gone home for the holidays. So when I touched down in Crimea I was feeling extremely isolated and desperately in need of some encouraging fellowship. God apparently knew that in advance and used Jerry Perkins and his crew to send out a little reminder of what Paul wrote in Philippians 4:19, *"And my God will meet all your needs according to His glorious riches in Christ Jesus."* In fact, speaking of encouraging fellowship, the Russian/Ukrainian team, after their time with me, traveled to Chechnaya to minister temporarily. Their goal was more along the lines of humanitarian work since the needs were so great in the midst of the fighting. Yuri, Oleg, Casha, Roma, and Andre, along with the others, really quelled my doubts about being exactly where God wanted me. "With Russians and Ukrainians like these guys," I thought to myself, "there is still a lot of hope for this fallen world." God used their tremendous faith to minister to me at just the right time. Meanwhile, during their stay in Chechnaya, I was receiving intermittent reports on their progress as well as all the juicy stories of the bombings and gunfire they bore witness to, which was just added support for me. It all forced me to keep my own situation in the proper perspective by keeping me fairly humble throughout, while also preparing me for what lay ahead.

There were still some empty feelings about everything. The loneliness was probably one of the biggest factors; but I did have a Russian hostess to talk to. Her name was Olga and she spoke English almost fluently. We had lots of interesting discussions. Olga's only daughter had moved to Israel, leaving her with a very antisocial husband to deal with all by her lonesome. Therefore, when I entered the picture, both of our needs for companionship were met instantly. But her need for chatting had long been an issue, making her almost overbearing at times. I got the impression that I was standing in for her long lost daughter and that's something I couldn't take for long. Add to that the fact that I quickly developed the worst coughing spree of my life. Within three weeks' time, I was back in Dubke, finally beginning to feel at home for a change.

After several months in Dubke, already adjusting well, I heard that the KGB had been looking for me. They found out that I was no longer at Olga's place, but rather in Dubke. Well, since I was trying to renew my six-month visa, this presented a sticky little problem. The government was not pleased with my elusiveness and we were concerned about the potential repercussions. "Lord," I prayed, "I'm finally starting to feel comfortable here in Crimea. I realize that I unwittingly made a mistake here, but you won't let them deport me when I'm just getting started, will you?" My emotional skepticism resurfaced, causing me to wonder whether this whole plan of mine was just that: MY PLAN. Was this all just a big mistake? Stress pushed me to pray more than usual and, while I didn't check my email this time, I did consult my desk calendar.

At that time, I had a calendar on my desk that emphasized a specific passage of Scripture for each day. Admittedly, I'd been neglecting it for some time, but God rapidly rekindled that desire because I was getting rather desperate for a sign from Him. Hollywood actor Tim Allen says that freewill is not just an illusion. His take is that we're all stand-up comics with a catch: God writes the joke but lets us choose the punch line. I'm sure glad that Tim's an actor and not a preacher. Either way, joke or no joke, this particular one wasn't to my liking. So I gave the punch-line privileges back to God this time. Here's what God had to say through my desk calendar on that particular day: *"Do not be afraid, keep on speaking, do not be silent. For I am with you, and no one is going to attack or harm you, because I have many people in this city" (Acts 18:9-10).* In that passage, Paul was in fear for his life in the city of Corinth. He was even contemplating a possible escape from the city until the Lord comforted him through the use of a vision. Despite our differing circumstances, God's comfort was applicable to both of us. I felt as though God had lifted my burden and I was ecstatic because my visa problem literally resolved itself over night. What's more amazing is that the following verse indicates that the apostle stayed in Corinth for an additional year and a half, wholly confident of God's will. In my case, there is a striking parallel because this all occurred at the six-month marker of my two-year commitment to Crimea, also leaving me with a year and a half to serve in confidence. And that's basically what happened, but there's still much to tell.

David Hollowell, a fellow missionary in Crimea, once quipped, "You know John, in some ways your ministry to Tatars reminds me a little of the apostle Paul's. But, to be honest, John, *you're definitely no apostle Paul!*" Well, you can say that again! In fact, I probably have more in common with Tim Allen. Sorry about that Tim.

Chapter Fourteen
This just can't all be for nothing!

It was around that time that I attended Miriam's birthday party, where I met Delavir, a physics major at the local university. Delavir, though fully aware of my intentions concerning the Muslim community, seemed surprisingly amiable, his grandfather having been an Islamic sheik notwithstanding. Perhaps that was because the party itself could probably have even convinced Hamas to set aside its differences temporarily. Don Tingle, a professor of Islam at an American seminary, was also present with his two teenage sons.

There were many highlights. One of the funniest was when a Muslim neighbor, who dominated the conversation with a limitless barrage of irrelevant questions, thanks to his level of intoxication, began serenading us with some lengthy Tatar song that many of us still think he made up on the spot. The song was unintelligible, our new friend was almost unconscious, and we were a bit unprepared for what happened next. Don, unlike his sons, tried valiantly to contain his laughter by modestly sipping his tea. Since our way-under-the-influence Tatar entertainer was busy singing at the top of his lungs and I was hiding behind Don's sons who were laughing uncontrollably, none of us noticed that Don had been choking on a piece of bread for the last two minutes. Seeing that he was almost blue in the face and about the keel over on us, we swiftly attended to him. Danny, one of Don's sons, began slapping Dad on the back in hopes that that would improve the situation, which just made things worse. In the end, Don came through it all like a champ, just as our Tatar friend was finishing one of his greatest hits, absolutely oblivious to what was happening around him. He even decided to call poor Don on the carpet for not showing proper respect during his debut. Needless to say, we were all relieved that it wasn't Don's birthday celebration. Furthermore, Miriam's composure and overall demeanor really impressed me, all things considered. Regarding her Tatar neighbor, Miriam turned to me, smiling from ear to ear, and remarked, "You know, he's ruining my party!" Yep, indeed, and what a party it was!

Delavir instantly became one of my best friends, taking a weighty interest in my beliefs and work, despite his claims as a purported atheist. In time, he also began attending our church in Crimea, professing to everybody that John had induced within him an authentic belief in God. I was excited about the slew of fresh possibilities. Inordinate chunks of time was spent with him so that he'd become our first Muslim convert to Christianity. I also planned to eventually have him spearhead the majority of our efforts in the Muslim community. I invested fifteen whole months, both cultivating our daily relationship and strengthening Delavir's newfound faith, which eventually included a belief in Jesus Christ as Lord and Savior. One of my most memorable experiences with Delavir was at his home where he referred to Christ as the one true God. He even referred to Jesus as, "my personal Redeemer," in front of his mother and sister. That moment will forever linger in my memory. It was a strange moment for me because I almost felt that my ears were playing tricks on me. I had never heard him say that before and my astonishment almost jostled me into a suspicion mode for which I felt a tad guilty. Consequently, coupled with my euphoria was a nagging uncertainty that really started to bug me.

Delavir's family was very poor and, since he had asked for a handout a couple of times, I knew that ulterior motives played some sort of role in our relationship. In my book that was forgivable, though, as long as he continued seeking the truth in God's book. Delavir regularly began staying with us at my host family's apartment. His family lived way out of town, so getting there after dark was a real chore without a car. Since he had classes in the morning he would often spend the night at our pad, which occasionally included supper and breakfast. Unfortunately, the money and accommodation issues were not the only ones bothering me. Overall, Delavir was a fairly nice guy but he did have some selfish idiosyncrasies. Some might even say they were duplicitous traits. For example, after staying with us regularly for approximately three months, seldom thanking my Russian hostess for feeding him, we discovered that he had been using our toothbrushes the entire time. We were all pretty offended, and disgusted, to put it mildly, and it wouldn't be long before things would come to a head, transforming one of my best friends into one of my best enemies.

At that time, we had just begun assembling an international group of Christians from America, South Africa, Russia, Ukraine, and Uzbekistan, in order to develop a cultural program for our Crimean Tatar friends at a local Christian café. It ran like clockwork every Monday evening at 5 pm and we'd simply get to know each other informally, sitting on the rug with coffee and refreshments. We would usually raise a specific non-threatening cultural issue that inevitably would drum up some friendly deliberation, given our cultural diversity. It was fun. At times it was even beneficial. I recall one question that really spurred on some discussion: "What aspect of your culture do you value most?" Although I was probably thinking about Pamela Anderson at that point, which was a mistake because she's actually Canadian *(I'm joking of course)*, the freedom of religion was my answer. "Granted," I explained, "it's certainly not perfect freedom, but it is the original basis upon which America was born. And I'm sincerely grateful for that!" That immediately stirred the interest of the Muslims who were present because that notion was foreign to them. "How do you think you'd feel having complete freedom to choose your spiritual beliefs?" I asked them.

The consensus they came to seemed like more of a revelation to them than it was to us: "We don't know how to answer that question because we can't even imagine having that kind of freedom." I remember that some bridges were built that evening because many Tatars started asking questions about their culture that they'd never posed before, and while we were all exhilarated by the latest headway being made, behind the scenes was one conspicuous individual in the crowd who was becoming increasingly rancorous. His name was Delavir.

The following Monday had my curiosity levels in the stratosphere because I was wondering who else would join us at the café from the Tatar community. "Curiosity killed the cat," regrettably, as they say. There were neither fatalities nor felines involved, but I sure learned a hard lesson about being careful for what I wished for. I was hoping we'd have a larger crowd and that objective was met smoothly, but that's just about all that went smoothly that evening. Delavir, in pretending to advance our cause by inviting a bunch of new visitors, deliberately sabotaged our work by bringing along ten fanatical Muslims. They weren't exactly the visitors we were hoping to see. There were four main instigators. Sayeet was from Sudan, Jihad *(Holy War)* was from Egypt, Servine was a Crimean Tatar studying Arabic at the local mosque, and Ali Muhammad *(Oleg)* represented the Russian Islamic community. Well, they had no intention of letting our cultural program continue, and therefore purposely created enough tension to scare off most of the folks we had successfully befriended. Before the evening concluded, we had forever lost over half of our regulars. And, instead of our typical light conversation over tea, for the next three months we were now grudgingly obligated to engage in heated theological/political debates with several acrimonious zealots. In contrast to pleasantly collaborating with Youth With A Mission, we were fed the unwelcome task of confronting "Radicals With A Mission" head on.

A suitable excerpt from my journal verbally recounts my melancholy cynicism. However, due to my brand new desk calendar, which provided a daily quote from various Christian authors, it also offers a promising window of hope for my clouded perspective at that stage in the game:

> "Delavir is beginning to undermine my work. The one Tatar who I thought would continue my work turned out to be a traitor. It is not definite yet, but likely. He's begun hanging with some conservative Muslims and actually showed an Ahmad Dedat debate and Muslim propaganda

to a Tatar I've been trying to reach for Jesus Christ after our cultural program last night. He got angry with me last night and shouted at me because of my refusal to accept the authority of the Qur'an. He wanted to argue about it but I refused to because of his demeanor, reminding him that we were friends, not enemies. 'Delavir,' I reminded him, 'I've helped your family! I've helped you! And now you want to create tension between us? You're acting like we're enemies right now but I don't want to be your enemy!' I think he felt a bit sorry for what he said and things calmed down some. Nevertheless, we're going opposite directions at this point. I've spent so much time with him . . . maybe in vain.

After our little squabble, I came home thinking I was totally helpless, not knowing exactly what to do. I finally decided to look at my small Christian desk calendar for the first time since June 29th and this is what Charles Colson wrote: 'When the frustration of my helplessness seemed greatest, I discovered God's grace was more than sufficient. After my imprisonment, I could look back and see how God used my powerlessness for His purposes. What He has chosen for my most significant witness was not my triumphs or victories, but my defeat' *(Colson and Santilli, 1987, p. 273).*"

Approximately two and a half months later, during Ramadan, I showed up at the Christian café for our Monday evening program only to find this hostile group performing its Muslim prayer rituals for all Christian onlookers to behold. This was happening inside the Christian café so we were all basically afforded no other option than to patiently dillydally while they finished their agenda, before we could start ours. I think we waited for about forty-five minutes or so. I had long felt that this group was rudely overstepping its bounds, but this stunt infuriated me because, although we were winning the debates, it still seemed like we were steadily losing ground. Not only did I sense that we were beating the air, but I also felt like we were often on the defensive inside our own fortress. And that disturbed me! So, I instinctively decided to alter our card for the evening for the sake of channeling some of our disgust in a more positive direction.

"Okay people, let's do something different tonight," I suggested. "Why don't we play some fun games and get better acquainted for a change? All we ever do is argue with each other but that's not too productive by itself. I believe that striving to develop more healthy relationships here will foster openness and objectivity regarding the truth, as well as helping us to love and respect one another as people made in God's own image. Remember, we are supposed to love each other regardless of what we believe, right?"

Sayeet, after sarcastically rolling his eyes, flatly dismissed my suggestion, creating a dialectic decor by promptly raising several contentious issues to dispute.

"Come on already!" I protested.

"No!" he asserted. "We're not here to play games! We're here to get to the truth! The most important thing is doing what God wants!"

Cutting him off with a raised voice, I finally spoke my mind: "No! The most important thing is not doing what God wants! The most important thing is doing what I want because this is my program and this is our building. And if you don't like it then you can take a flying leap!" So much for that loving each other option, huh?

Within a couple of weeks, even the extremists were admitting that a truce was essentially the only viable recourse. After dishing out their entire arsenal, they were forced to retreat because our war morphed into a simple game of Tic-Tac-Toe. Everyone's mind was immovably fixed; nobody was crossing over to the other side. Just as the pack appeared out of nowhere, they vanished without a trace, taking Delavir with them. In fact, my last memory of Delavir came from one of their final appearances at the café. During Ramadan we all sat down to argue. While all the Christians were chomping on cookies, the other side was salivating because the sun had not completely set yet. *(During fasts, Muslims are only allowed to eat after sundown.)*

Anya, one of our Christian apologists, offered Delavir a cookie and he wontedly snatched it without even thinking. Just as he was in the process of swallowing his free morsel, Anya queried, "Delavir, are you not celebrating Ramadan this year?" According to the radicals' testimonies, breaking with the fast's regulations, even once, requires the transgressor to serve a seventy-year sentence in hell to atone for his sinful negligence. Delavir mutely cowered in the corner the rest of the evening without offering up so much as a cough, let alone a word. His horrifying facial expression spoke volumes though. In any case, losing Delavir was a bittersweet blessing that emotionally took its toll on me because all of the time and effort I invested in him, to my dejection, just wound up creating a monster.

Indeed, it was hard looking on the bright side after all that had gone on during those three very draining months, but some good did come out of it all. First, those debates taught me a great deal about Islam while underscoring some of the key questions that Muslims were asking about Christianity. As a result, I was inspired to write a book for both Muslims, as well as Christians interested in working with them, which is still building bridges between both religious communities on the Crimean Peninsula and beyond. Secondly, several Christians were prompted to consider further ministry involvement among Muslim people groups. Anya subsequently spent time in the US studying Islam at a Christian seminary and has ministered to Muslims in Azerbaijan, Crimea, and Moldova. She's also currently studying Arabic at a university in Iran. Finally, at least two spectators from our "Monday Night Fights" gradually became convinced of the need to accept Jesus Christ, as opposed to embracing their Islamic roots more keenly. They were my acquaintances who happened to be non-practicing Muslims from the Tatar community. They were the only ones who remained with our peaceful cultural program even when it turned confrontational and threatening. And, in my opinion, they were the true heroes in all of this because they were risking more than any of us by simply attending. When you meet them, shortly, you'll see how their faith and courage increased after their eventual conversions.

In the meantime, I had also been developing some strong friendships in the Muslim villages. In fact, both Russian/Ukrainian and Danish YWAM teams helped me to lay a couple of floors in one of the homes there, in addition to assisting with other fairly demanding construction projects. We centered the majority of our efforts in two homes. One was located in the village of Belaya, while the other was across the highway in Kominka. Both villages are situated on the outskirts of Simferopol, Ukraine. In Belaya, we had flying-colored success on two fronts: 1) the construction work, and 2) establishing meaningful rapport with the people. Our best contact was in Belaya with a fun couple, Setholi and Gulnara. In fact, Setholi gladly accepted the Bible we had offered him and frequently reminded me, throughout the first year of my subsequent contact with him, that he was reading it regularly. Setholi was a gentle man who seemed extremely open to the truth. In addition to that, he genuinely loved his wife and two girls dearly. But Setholi, now an invalid due to an unfortunate accident he survived two years earlier, was neither able to earn enough to feed his family nor physically capable of finishing his own construction efforts on their home. And, although his depression was severe, his sanguine personality helped to disguise it well. Nevertheless, whenever time permitted, I made it my goal to encourage him in any way possible, being afforded the chance to observe first-hand how he handled his rigorous responsibilities from day to day. I was optimistic, especially since he evidently continued searching for God's heart in all of this.

So, even though Delavir seemed to officially be out of the picture at that point, I still had great ambitions for the villages in which we were laboring. Setholi clearly stood out in my mind as a spiritual beacon for the community, as did another family who I'd been visiting regularly. In fact, this other Tatar family not only invited me to conduct private studies in their home but they even attended a Christian program at the local movie theater, subsequently extending an invitation for me to join them the following night.

"What's wrong with this picture?" I thought. "I'm a Christian missionary and my Muslim friends are inviting me to church with them!" I had spent immoderate chunks of time with their large family, and to this day, as I reflect back on my time with all of them, I still believe that they were genuinely open to the gospel. Regrettably, Delavir had joined me on several occasions in order to visit with them too, giving him a foot in the door. That came back to haunt me because Delavir would later destroy my relationship with their family by maintaining contact with them and warning against the potential aftermath of any further invitations they granted me. They immediately admitted their fears of the locals, the mosque across the street, and the fact that word was getting out about our studies. So we were forced to call it quits. Several henchmen from the local mosque even paid them an impromptu visit, which really drove the point home. I distinctly recall not only feeling doubly betrayed at that juncture, but also experiencing a bit of nervous tension myself. My number of visits to their home waned rapidly, as did any glimmer of hope I formerly held out for that family. Thus, with Delavir's double double-crossing affecting every nook and cranny of my life and work, from my toothbrush, to my interpersonal relationships, to my faith in God, my mind couldn't help but begin drawing up the blueprints for an accident-waiting-to-happen that carried with it the potential of toppling my spirit altogether.

Luckily, all of this took place during my second year in Crimea, following my first scheduled furlough. Ah, that saving stretch at home with family and friends, though transitory, rejuvenated my spirit enough to enable me to face these pending disparagements with enough fortitude and stamina to weather these storms without seeing my faith wholly decimated. Just as a mission trip can change one's life, a furlough can save one's faith. Still, I must confess that I was shaken up enough to wonder whether I was only called to Crimea for the purpose of being God's whipping boy, while fully ruling out any possibility that He was literally working in and through me with a designated plan that was remotely advantageous. Initially I assumed, in spite of the rough start in Crimea, that God had a definite plan for my life and labor there. However, that attitude began to change drastically when this "will of God thing," as I formerly called it, turned out to be a major drag, outwardly lacking any foreseeable redeeming or intrinsic purpose whatsoever. I didn't lose my faith in God but I did begin questioning whether God wanted me there, especially inasmuch as there still would be other ingredients poured in the mix.

Before my CPR *(i.e. furlough)*, while visiting with the family who would eventually get cold feet on account of Delavir's influence, Setholi unexpectedly dropped by. That usually would have been a pleasant surprise for all of us, and this time was no different, except for the fact that we were just sitting down for dinner. Nevertheless, his ostensibly urgent request, for some reason, couldn't seem to wait: "Friends, I'd really like for you all to come by my house for a little while, as soon as possible. I've got several things I'd like to say to you all. I'd really appreciate it if you'd give me just a few minutes of your time." Well, we all got ourselves together in record time, leaving dinner in the oven on warm, and made our brief trek over to Setholi's. Upon arrival, although his wife was all smiles, nobody failed to recognize that she'd been weeping at some point. Naturally, Setholi's vigorously upbeat disposition, as always, misled everyone into thinking that life was nothing shy of pristine.

Setholi, while holding the Bible we had given him, addressed our group of about twenty or so, all scrunched up in his tiny living room. I almost got the impression that he had prepared a sermon or personal testimony for us. The crowd's curiosity had reached its saturation point as we all listened intently on the edge of our seats. He started out with his wife Gulnara, by apologizing for all of the times he had offended her.

Tears flowed freely as she interrupted with words of consolation, "Setholi, I love you! When have you ever hurt my feelings? I can't even remember the last time that happened. I don't even understand why you're doing this. Can't you tell how much you mean to me?" Her words seemed to make little difference to him because he was determined to express his regret for all the heartache he had caused her throughout their years together.

Then he turned to his children to continue asking for forgiveness. Setholi covered everybody in that room, tearfully communicating the anguish in his soul due to his negligence as a father, a husband, a neighbor, a friend, and even as a man. After opening his Bible, he motioned to me saying, "John, I also want to tell you how much you mean to me for all of the loving care you've shown all of us, especially my family. I will never forget that my friend! I don't know if I have ever hurt you in any way, but if so, I want to take this opportunity to tell you how sorry I am. I also want to let you know how thankful I am to you for giving me this book because it's shown me how sinful I've been throughout the course of my life. People may argue and say that I've never hurt them before, and they may even have a case, but nobody can deny the fact that I've caused God tremendous grief throughout the years. And, for that, I am exceedingly sorrowful. There's just an abysmal sense of guilt in my soul that I don't know how to dissolve, no matter what I do or how much I pray!" He then proceeded to express his gratitude to all of us for the chance to speak his mind, ending his talk by requesting our continued support, before bidding us farewell.

Since the crowd was at a loss as to what to say, except for a few comments from his wife about the need to talk to a professional counselor, I expeditiously interjected some of my sentiment. Rather than corroborating his wife's words, I proceeded to openly preach a sermon on grace. I even had Setholi read an appropriate passage from Romans to clarify my convictions. As Setholi, still gripping his Bible, accompanied me on our walk out to the main road, since it was already getting late, I hugged him and told him how much I respected him for sharing his deepest feelings with us. "Setholi," I concluded, "I'm leaving for America in just a few days. But I won't be stateside very long. So take care of yourself, keep reading that book in your hand, look to Him whenever you have the chance, and look to see me very soon!" Sadly, that was the last time I would ever see Setholi. What I had interpreted as a testimonial-like spiritual cry for help was actually an attempt at putting his house in order. For my friend, Setholi, the pressures of his new handicap, now depriving him of the ability to adequately support his family's needs, became a burden too heavy for him to carry.

Setholi's suicide, coupled with everything else that would come to pass during that second year in Crimea, almost became too much for me to bear also. After the wieldy languishing effect of this smack in the face, I wasn't contemplating any self-destructive behavior or anything like that, but I was ruminating over the need for a total metamorphosis concerning the general direction of my life. In the midst of all this speculative suspicion, however, stood a gnawing intuition - *you might call it "faith"* - blaring out at me: "THIS JUST CAN'T ALL BE FOR NOTHING!"

Chapter Fifteen
Take it like a man and just believe!

☙◦❧

Sometime after my furlough, there was yet another incident that probably gave me whatever it took to make it through that second year, regardless of the roadblocks. Though the KGB had ordered me out of Dubke at the six-month marker, during year number one, I still maintained contact with my former Tatar host family there. In fact, we had agreed to have dinner together once a week, allowing us to reminisce and laugh a lot. On one particular occasion, though, we didn't do very much of either because of some alarming news, which was much more than just a smack in the face.

My former hostess greeted me at the door with a somberly startled look and decided to get straight to the point: "John, what I'm about to tell you is very serious! So please don't take it lightly! Two days ago, a man from the central mosque came to my house. I'd never met him before and I'm not exactly sure what his intentions were, but he is apparently a very influential leader in Simferopol's Muslim community. He has a lot of connections and can evidently make people vanish without ever having to answer for it. To tell you the truth, I'm pretty concerned for my family's welfare because he knows exactly what you're doing in the Muslim villages. He even told me, John, that if you decide to continue visiting those villages, then he won't be surprised if you're the next one to disappear. So, if I were you, I would either start praying like never before or seriously consider a job change!"

Changing my vocation, frankly speaking, sounded like an excellent suggestion, all things considered. Ironically, I couldn't bring myself to accept that after all of my efforts. Some folks would have automatically concluded that, given the fact that there was no tangible fruit after a year and a half of ministry, especially in light of the gloomy scene, that a job change wasn't just the preferable option but the only one. My viewpoint, to the contrary, differed probably because I flatly refused to believe that I had experienced monumental discouragement, excessive grief, a loss of about 550 days of my life, severe testing of my faith, and life-threatening episodes, all for nothing. I was practically starting to feel like Elijah, whom God sent to a brook that dried up *(1 Kings 17)*. Also, as in the prophet's case, there still remained a fraction of hope whispering, "Relief is coming!" In a sense, I almost think that my faith was joined by those last remaining strands of pride within me, provoking me to stubbornly dig my heels in and pray rather than waving the white flag. Nope, I wasn't about to be defeated that easily.

God would later alleviate me of the jolts of my woes, doing so, not surprisingly, in a customarily wry fashion for which He's so renowned. And in the next chapter you'll see how. During that drought in Israel, when Elijah ran out of water, the Lord took care of his need but not before the prophet acquired a nice case of cottonmouth *(1 Kings 17:10)*. What do you think Elijah thought when God sent him to a woman, with the promise of food and drink, only to hear her say, *"I don't have any bread---only a handful of flour in a jar and a little oil in a jug. I am gathering a few sticks to take home and make a meal for myself and my son, that we may eat it---and die." (v.12)*? Elijah, desperately searching for any available mitigating circumstances, is sent to somebody who has already given up hope altogether.

However, thanks to the durability of Elijah's faith, it doesn't seem to impact him much. *Elijah still believed!* And they all survived without a hitch, that is, until the lady's son suddenly stopped breathing, inciting her to blame the prophet. See, she was already in her state of denial. "True," she conceded, "Elijah's here and he is doing some eyebrow-raising slide of hand that's even getting some grub on the table for a change. And that's a welcomed reprieve, granted, but in the long run it doesn't matter because we're all doomed anyway!" Her faith, like Elijah's brook, had dried up; her faith had failed her. She had already made her decision. No more believing; no more quick-fix it tricks. "That's it!" she confidently sighed. "Game over!" Elijah, on the other hand, was another story altogether. He wasn't throwing in the towel just yet. The results? Well, by the end of the chapter, we not only see a physical resurrection in the boy's life, but also a spiritual resurrection in hers. "I guess it's not over after all!" she shouted, finally exuding with a peppy little get-up-and-go-like enthusiasm that had long been replaced with the typical gloom and doom. Once God got behind the wheel, her life and attitude took a radical turn. Finally, there was faith in the miraculous, hope despite her helplessness, and a racy new sports car in her driveway, called: *"some zest for life."*

Similarly, Elijah was on top of Rhapsody Mountain, but it wouldn't be long before he'd be on top of Mount Carmel *(1 Kings 18)*. Oh, at the summit everything works out just fine, but as he makes his descent we see that life's cookie crumbles in a flash. Even before we wrap up the following chapter, Elijah's looking like that widow before the resurrection. In fact, his suds were so pronounced that he began hoping for the Grim Reaper to show up *(1 Kings 19:4)*. The Author of Life, however, shows up instead. The twist here, of course, is that God never allowed the prophet's wish to come true. As you recall, Elijah got swept up to heaven without ever experiencing death *(2 Kings 2:11)*, which is just another example of how God does much better than granting our every wish.

As you might have already guessed, just as Elijah's intense drive subsided to a halt, mine would too. Incidentally, all throughout the account of Elijah's ministry, we see God asking him the same question repeatedly: *"Elijah, what are you doing here?"* And that's something I definitely began asking myself.

All of this reminds me of the Mononucleosis I caught in Crimea, back in 1998. That bout, just like this one, almost permanently knocked me out of Ukraine. At first, we weren't sure what the problem was. Initially, I just assumed it was the flu so I hibernated for about two weeks until I couldn't stand it anymore. Then it became plain to see that this illness was a bit more serious. Some of my symptoms looked like hepatitis, so I checked into the hospital and was given a room in that wing. Having never been admitted into a Ukrainian hospital before, I wasn't sure what to expect. Not only did I feel terrible, but I also felt helpless and scared because my life was now in the hands of a few Ukrainian doctors with purely Ukrainian remedies. Moreover, the place was just filthy. I even asked the cleaning lady if I could possibly take a cold sponge bath and she said, "Oh, are you kidding me? I wouldn't! I mean, look at how dirty that tub is!" When the cleaning lady complains, you know you're in trouble!

Since it was a hepatitis unit, my friends were prohibited from visiting me. Fortunately, we were on the ground floor, permitting us to have some contact through the window, despite the metal bars covering it. Sometimes I felt like I was in a penitentiary rather than a hospital. Plus, I was getting shots in the rear end with Ukrainian needles filled with some mysterious Ukrainian . . . stuff. Well, I only lasted three days before my escape. My friends had informed me that once they made a definite diagnosis, there would be no escaping. In other words, once a diagnosis is made, you're stuck there. For me, that was a rather convincing argument. Needless to say, I made the most of my fleeting opportunity and got the heck out of there. In fact, at that point, I even made a decision to get the heck out of Ukraine for good. I had to return to America to get the antibiotics needed for my recovery anyway, so that just seemed like the best way to kill two birds with one stone. After some time in the States, though, I was able to heal and clear my mind some. I came to understand that crazy circumstances sometimes cause us to make crazy choices. Nope, God wasn't calling me home after all.

One reason why my illness was so difficult to diagnose was because the symptoms I had were extremely rare. Not only were the platelets in my blood being wracked, but painful boils were beginning to appear on areas of my body. I was generally able to handle the majority of them with hot baths and compresses, but then there was one that just didn't want to cooperate. It just kept growing in size and sensitivity. So my Russian host family decided to take me to the clinic to lance and drain it. Unfortunately, the clinic happened to be on one of those back roads in Ukraine, which means more potholes than asphalt. "Whoever masterminded these roads," I screamed from the passenger seat, "obviously wasn't thinking about people with furuncles on their backsides! . . . Ouch! I think it just burst!" When I finally got on my tummy, the doctor made a comment about the size of the boil, telling the nurse to increase the level of Novocain. Well, he quickly turned to me and began telling me a joke. "Yep," I thought, "I'm in big trouble!"

We finally got home with no painkillers and the Novocain wearing off. Luda, my hostess, read my mind about the need for some pills. Before heading out to get some, they told me it would take about forty-five minutes. "Give me some vodka instead!" I insisted.

"Well," came back the response, "that's an idea, but if you drink then you won't be able to take any painkillers." Well, I decided to wait it out and take it like a man. *What was I thinking?* Since us men have a much lower tolerance for pain, I indeed took it rather fittingly. The neighbors were probably wondering whether or not to call the cops. I just stuck my face in the pillow and yelled, screamed, and moaned, like only a real man can. That went on for about a good half hour or so. I even thought of Christ on the cross and vividly remember shouting "Jesus, I can't believe you did it!" about twenty times. I don't think I've ever been that spiritual in my life! After the ordeal, I emailed my father and told him the entire story. "John," he answered, "we all think that you're a real man for not drinking the vodka, but if I'd been in your shoes . . . well, anyway."

A couple of days later, the doctor extracted the little cylinder he had inserted for the purpose of draining out the dead white blood cells. That was also pleasant, especially since he couldn't get it until the third or fourth attempt. The next day, which was actually the first day I had been able to get outside and walk around with some sense of triumphant peace and serenity, being the victorious warrior-like man I had proved to be, I was taking a nice calm stroll near our apartment building. Just then, some toddler came out of nowhere, running past me at full tilt. Is that all? No. He was erratically waving his arms, as he ran, subsequently socking me in a very sensitive spot. Did he stop to console me? No, he just kept running with his hands waving, totally oblivious to all the physical and psychological damage for which he was responsible. However, I am not bitter! I promise!

Chapter Sixteen
The only contingency plan that works

○○○

Well, how did God help me handle my former hostess' frightening monition? It was approximately eighteen months after my arrival in Crimea. My desk calendar, containing a daily Bible verse, had already been in the trash bin for some time. But I still had a journal that was continually being compiled on my laptop. I rarely, if ever, browsed through it since it was generally designated for future use. I figured that someday it might come in handy if I ever chose to write a book like this one. I obviously pegged that one, but I never expected it to help me in other ways. They say that if you keep a journal you'll keep yourself. I agree. In fact, the majority of this book came straight out of my journal, which represents much of my personal testimony. So journaling is great stuff indeed! At the same time, by journaling, you often give God a chance to teach you a thing or two as you read it later on. God may even work a tiny wonder into your life that way.

In the midst of all I had been enduring, and was yet to digest, I was virtually starving for yet another one of those propelling nudges in faith's direction. I really needed a sign. For two weeks, after my former hostess dropped the bomb, I prayed harder than I'd ever prayed in my entire life. After all, it was either my ministry that was on the line, OR MY VERY LIFE! "Lord," I prayed, "what do you want me to do? Please show me your will!" In my heart, I'd resolutely determined that if God failed to convince me, during those fourteen days, to continue my efforts in the Muslim villages, then His will for my life was clearly somewhere else on the planet. And that *"somewhere else"* was looking a lot like the United States of America because, even though I was in my mid-twenties, I still wanted my Mommy!

Selfishly peeking outside of God's will became both effortless and even enjoyable because that represented my frail attempts at getting even with the Almighty. These God-lessons were starting to irritate me more than ever and my former antagonistic arrogance, which was now melting down into more of a defense mechanism, returned in the form of an arctic callousness that inundated my prayer life. "Lord," I griped, "I'm sacrificing my best years for you and my life is falling apart. I know you're the Creator and all, but I'm exasperated! And I'm aggravated too! In fact, I almost feel unjustly exploited here. And now, if that weren't enough, my life's in danger! Where are you, and why aren't you doing something?"

Please excuse the feeble analogy, but in some sense I actually sounded like Moses, whose prayers also toted a tendency to put God on the spot from time to time. His circumstances, admittedly, were a bit more trying than mine, and unlike yours truly, Moses still retained enough spiritual discipline to demonstrate remarkable evidence of an unfailing dose of faithful humility. Moses, who lived 1,500 years before the birth of Christ, clearly had a better handle on Christ's teachings than I did. He realized that any credible attempt at following Christ's example would not only require getting out of one's comfort zone, but also doing so with the proper attitude regardless. "John," Christ doubtless thought to Himself, "don't you remember what I said about counting the cost in Luke 14? So please don't get peeved at me because of your lack of faith!" My egomaniacal disposition also precluded me from hearing Him whisper Hebrews 12:3-5: *"Consider Him who endured such opposition from sinful men, so that you will not grow weary and lose heart. In your struggle against sin, you have not yet resisted to the point of shedding your blood. And you have forgotten that word of encouragement."*

While still in the Communist death camp, Alexander Solzhenitsyn decided to end his suffering by running away from a guard. He planned to take a bullet in the back and instantly put an end to all of his misery because he was convinced that God, like the rest of the world, had forgotten all about him. "All hope is lost!" he thought. But just as Casha *(i.e. Alexander)* was preparing to make his mad dash, another prisoner approached him. The man looked intently into his eyes, with a facial expression that silently cried out: "Casha, I love you!" Although verbal communication was forbidden in the camp, that stare spoke volumes. Just then, the prisoner drew the shape of a cross on the ground, evermore diverting Casha from his suicidal tendencies. Three days later, they were all freed and sent to Geneva, Switzerland. God remembered Casha's pain, He remembers yours, and He would soon prove to remember mine too.

Immanuel Kant claimed that the three greatest motivators for man are: duty, desire, and love. While the Bible perfectly combines these three incentives for us, in Christianity's purest form, by keeping a wholesome balance between them, sometimes we also need a small miracle in order to keep us in God's backyard. Toward the end of those two weeks, when I was on the verge of making some rash decisions about closing up shop and heading home, a strange thought invaded my brain: "Start reading your journal!" So I did. And that's when I ran across God's ten-second sermon about the KGB episode, from a year earlier, which, yet again, smacked me upside the head: *"One night the Lord spoke to Paul in a vision: 'Do not be afraid; keep on speaking, do not be silent. For I am with you, and no one is going to attack and harm you, because I have many people in this city'" (Acts 18:9-10).*

God wonderfully used my journal not only to remind me of His desire to be **closer** to me, but also to show me how **close** He already was. The Psalmist's narration correlates well: *"I cried out to God for help; I cried out to God to hear me. When I was in distress, I sought the Lord; at night I stretched out my untiring hands and my soul refused to be comforted... I remembered my songs in the night. My heart mused and my spirit inquired...'Has God forgotten to be merciful? Has He in anger withheld His compassion?'... Then I thought, 'To this I will appeal: the years of the right hand of the Most High.' I will* *remember the deeds of the Lord; yes, I will remember your miracles of long ago... You are the God who performs miracles" (Psalm 77:1-2, 6, 9-11, 14).* Falling into disbelief is oftentimes second nature for us and that's why we all constantly need to stay abreast of God's journal *(the Holy Scriptures)* in addition to our own.

Donna Cole relates the story of her friend who was planning to lose weight but needed some more incentive. So her friend prayed that God would somehow help her to get increasingly motivated. A few days later, a neighbor approached her with this comment, "Oh, you're expecting? Congratulations!" Looking up to heaven, she cried, "Ah, Lord, that was kind of harsh!" They always say that if you have to swallow a frog then don't stare at it very long and if you have to swallow more than one then start with the big ones first. After all the frogs I ingested, I felt like croaking. Like I said earlier, the center of God's will rarely lends itself to boredom. The paradox is that sometimes boredom seems more preferable, but usually not for very long. Either way, God's plan was working because I was again beginning to get roused about ministry. While that little reminder was more than enough to rekindle a fire in my belly for continuing the work, it wasn't enough to completely dissolve the bad taste in my mouth from all the frog legs I had consumed in the process. And adding to the slew of frog legs would be another nauseating dish on the way.

The nineteen-month marker invited a new John Murphy to come out and play. For conceivably the first time ever, I was actually fit for ministry. My ardor for service seemed balanced with an unavoidable sense of inadequacy. I couldn't help but feel helpless, which daily served up a healthy portion of humility and utter dependence on God. The problem was that I hadn't yet matured to the point of actually feeling comfortable with that. Although I esteemed the reality of my situation, especially with how it affected me in terms of my spiritual growth, it would only be a few months before boredom seemed like a much better option altogether.

Reflecting back on that reminds me of how I felt when I played three different roles in skits at Crimean-American College's Christmas program one year. Although the people who coaxed me into participating tried to convince me that my roles were crucial to

A Dumb American in a Strange Country

the success of their program, I swiftly grew quizzical when I found out that I would be playing a drunk, a mafia boss, and a homosexual, all in one day. Playing such meaningfully respectful roles pretty much spoke for itself, and closing in on the two-year marker, likewise, was the real kicker since my newfound humility was starting to resemble a self-conscious feeling of utter worthlessness instead.

Several years ago a friend and I stayed with a Christian woman in Zaporizhya, Ukraine, for a few days. In the course of our conversations we discovered that she sold Mary Kay products. Well, her boss took some soft lotion pads that they had just received and began rubbing her face and hands with them, raving about their scent and texture to everyone in the office: "Wow, these pads are so soft; they're just wonderful!" However, since the shipment was sent exclusively with English instructions, nobody knew what the pads were for. Thus, I was recruited to translate. You could just imagine how the boss must have felt when everyone realized that they were hemorrhoid pads, which describes how I felt after two years of being knocked off my high horse by consecutive traumatic sequences that produced absolutely no visible results from a ministry standpoint.

YWAM has a joke for its students, which is applicable for any missionary organization. Three people show up at the Judgment and each is given the right to ask one question after his sentencing. One is a Russian Orthodox monk who gets condemned to hell for hiding from people and their needs, so he asks: "God, why didn't you tell me that you didn't like that?" Then there's a Catholic man who, after being condemned to hell, asks: "Why didn't you tell me that praying to Mary was wrong?" Finally, after the YWAM missionary gets condemned to hell, he asks: "Okay, Lord, what exactly do you want me to learn from this experience?" Missionaries are trained to keep an eye out for any potential God-lessons, regardless of the situation, and some are able to do this fairly successfully. Then there are other missionaries, like me, who don't seem to thrive in this area very well.

After the Russian submarine, Kursk, went down, divers supposedly found a note that one of the servicemen had written: "Must not despair!" That sailor would have made some missionary. As for me, I had passed beyond both the point of despair and the God-lesson mode because I had come to believe that I'd erred in going to Crimea in the first place. I even began to find consolation in my surrender because it gave me a surefire escape route out of my situation.

"John," I reasoned, "it's pretty simple if you think about it! It's been two years and there are no conversions because you're not using your God-given talents. All you're doing is helping people with their physical needs, talking about Jesus from time to time, and trying to love them. But that's not enough because you're not teaching and preaching, which are your real strengths." Analyzing my viewpoint, in hindsight, makes me squeamish because it was still so steeped in that ugly arrogance-based defense mechanism. I claimed to believe in God but the kind of belief I possessed literally wound up making God dependent on me, instead of the other way around. I claimed to believe that it was God who builds His Church His way, but I obviously didn't because, in John's universe, John's talents were essential to God's success.

Let's be blunt for once. How can mere people, whose life spans only last for about seventy-five years or so, expect the Uncaused Cause to actually need something from them in order to function? Comparing our ability with God's is like comparing an amoeba's to man's. Can an amoeba land on the moon? Can man's abilities build God's Church? Now, some out there may be saying: "Wait a minute, John. God has specifically chosen to build His Church through our talents. For example, just look at Ephesians 4:11ff." Granted, we're to do our part until we mature, *"attaining to the whole measure of the fullness of Christ" (v.13)*. But let's not forget that it's only because of the one Spirit, one Lord, and one Father, getting it done in and through us in the preceding verses *(vv.4-6)*. That's why Jesus told us, in John 15:5, *"I am the Vine; you are the branches. If a man remains in me and I in him, he will bear much fruit; apart from me you can do nothing."*

In the final analysis, therefore, He's really the only One who brings the increase. God doesn't need our trivial talents to establish His Kingdom on Earth. God doesn't NEED anything, especially from us! As a matter of fact, we usually get in God's way with our talents and attitudes because He is frequently pushed aside and left in the wake of our shoestring achievements. In the real universe, however, which He created, by the way, God is building His Church in spite of us. In fact, in doing so He's actually building us up because we are His Church. *(The vast majority of us still need lots of work too.)* The most important aspect of that building process, from our vantage point, isn't based on something from which we may selfishly derive praise and glory for ourselves, such as in our "God-given" talents, but rather stems from the kind of authentic humility that comprehends and appreciates the potency of unswerving reliance upon Him. There is no greater sway in the universe than a deliberate contingency plan resting solely in the supernatural hands of the Living God. And, while I may have temporarily possessed that around the nineteen-month marker, by now it was long gone.

I used to teach English to a group in Ukraine. I once recall how a girl in my class asked an elementary question that raised a significant yet complex point that I had neglected to bring out, though she obviously wasn't even thinking along those lines. "Now, that's a GREAT question!" I declared. She looked rather bewildered, as I expected she would. Then another student, peering over in her direction just in time to notice her puzzled look, turned to me during the lull in the room and asked, "Ah, sir, are you sure about that one?" He, like me, knew that she didn't quite understand what she was asking. Turning to him, I quipped, "Well, that's another GREAT question!" Perhaps you're thinking: "John, I hear you, and I'm sure that the betrayal, the suicide, and the threats, must all have taken their toll on you. But after successfully weathering those storms, it's surprising how a mere lack of tangible results in the ministry could have ultimately defeated you." If you're thinking that way then you've got an excellent point whether you realize it or not.

You see, the fact that I was concentrating so much of my attention on the need for tangible results in my ministry immediately serves to suggest that my motives were impure. Throughout my trials, I failed to adequately guard my motives, allowing them to gradually become skewed. God has deliberately provided for us a system where we worship at least once a week so we can be reminded to protect God's priorities in our lives. The reason is because it doesn't take much time during the week to forget what our priorities should be and why. So gathering every few days is a critical reminder and encourager for all of us, and although I was assembling with other believers weekly, I was losing God's perspective. My poor attitude, when times got tough, gave Satan a chance to thwart any positive spiritual growth that might have otherwise taken root in my life. As they say, all the devil needs to dismantle our spiritual lives is an opportunity. Being the proud man I was, though, I was still determined to fulfill my two-year commitment to the field in order to avoid answering any discomforting questions upon my early arrival back at home. Hence, making good on my promise was a given, but "NEVER would I be grateful for the time I spent in Ukraine as a full-timer," I told myself, "nor would I ever return!" That stance immediately uncovers two God-lessons here: 1) never let selfishness take over because it can ruin your life, and 2) never ever say never again.

It wasn't long before I commenced with my departure plans, as well as plotting *"a new and improved"* direction for my life. Teaching, since that was my *"real gift,"* was selected as my manifest destiny, and history would be the subject. I had never really been much of a history buff, but I reckoned that time would change that if I set my mind to it. Before even applying to any universities, I had already narrowed my options down to two of them in Virginia: Lynchburg College and the College of William and Mary. "What a relief to have control over my life again!" I mused. It seemed like it had been an eternity since I had had a clear head with which to operate, but things were finally looking up. While I hadn't given up on God, I had given up on missionary service and the ministry in general.

Oh, incidentally, history wasn't just some random choice either. I had read enough to know, from the Christian authors especially, that there was a strong case for establishing God's influence over and involvement in history. Along those lines, the fact that America was leaning in the wrong direction made engaging in the debate pretty appealing to me. After all those debates with the Muslims, I guess you could say I was back in my arguing mood, primarily due to my bitterness. Sure, I was well aware that I would have to be very sensitive in the classroom about such things, but I was also convinced that I'd make a difference because I'd finally be using my teaching talents. How paradoxical was the fact that I determined to prove to the world the validity of God's actions throughout history, while completely rejecting any possibility that He was dynamically active within my own history! As you've probably guessed, though, God wasn't quite done putting the finishing touches on this particular chapter in my diary just yet.

Chapter Seventeen
Once there was a missionary who got saved . . .

～～

A couple of years ago, I was chosen to be the guest missionary speaker at a VBS program in Virginia. During the first day, a seven-year old boy who was sitting in front of me, turned around and asked: "Why do you have a mustache?" Well, apparently the cheap razor I used that day didn't quite give me the ideal close shave that most people prefer. I even noticed that myself on my way out the door that day.

Ungrateful for the reminder, I just replied, "Right, well, it happens."

Then he turned around again and said, "Ah, you do know that you're going bald too, right?"

"Yeah, yeah, that also happens!" I barked. "Now, can you turn around already?" Sometimes a little honesty is the last thing we need, but at other times it can actually change our lives forever.

It wasn't long before all my Russian friends knew about my plans to become a history teacher. It wasn't long before I started getting some feedback from them also. The general consensus from them was that, although I may not have been much of a missionary,

I would surely be a worse history teacher. "You might want to reconsider!" they advised.

A few days later, one of the leaders in our congregation, Misha Voshov, who was never known for his tact, pulled me aside and said, "John, I heard that you're leaving to go back home. Wow, that's a real shame since you haven't actually done anything! I mean, does that make any sense?"

Finally, there was an American teammate who was enthusiastically bent on giving me a piece of her mind. And she was determined to do it before I had the chance to exit the country with less than mortal wounds. But that chat more than deserves a new paragraph.

Earlier, we spoke briefly about Elijah and how God whisked him up to paradise first-class. Whoever said that the Wright Brothers were the first in flight at Kitty Hawk, North Carolina, were explicitly missing some vital information. Anyway, after Elijah's take off, Elisha became his successor. And let's just put it this way: LaVerne was to me what Elisha was to Hazael, in 2 Kings 8. There we see that Ben-Hadad, the king of Aram, had fallen ill. So he commissioned his helper, Hazael, to inquire of Elisha about whether or not he'd recover from his illness. Elisha, already privy to Hazael's plan to murder his master, freely divulged the details about a full recovery, while staring Hazael down like Mike Tyson would have in his prime, adding these words: *"But the Lord has revealed to me that he will in fact die" (2 Kings 8:10)*. Elisha's fixed gaze even made Hazael feel ashamed *(v. 11)*, but evidently not enough to prevent him from carrying out the strangling in verse fifteen. Well, you would have thought that I, like Hazael, had killing on the brain because of some of the looks LaVerne gave me, in the course of our meeting.

Elisha received a double portion of Elijah's spirit, which not only included the ability to raise the dead, but also the ability to put people in their place. Sometimes that even meant permanently. If you recall, in 2 Kings 1, we see how Elijah incinerated 102 men by calling fire down from heaven on them. Likewise, Elisha called two bears out of the woods to feast on 42 youths after they made fun of his receding hairline. Well, I was beginning to get the impression that my good friend, LaVerne, had received a triple portion of Elijah's spirit, if you know what I mean. She more than succeeded in putting me in my place. And, thanks to that one seemingly prophetic conversation, it also seems to have been permanently.

LaVerne started off like this: "You know, John, if you leave Ukraine you will never be at peace with that decision because you know in your heart of hearts that the only mission you may have satisfactorily completed is your own. I say that because there is just no legitimate way that you can sincerely claim any sense of accomplishment here whatsoever. I guess what I'm getting at, John, is the fact that, well, Misha's right! You *haven't* done anything! While you might have fulfilled your own goals, which were to dedicate two years of your life to God in Crimea, you've obviously forgotten all about God's goals in the process. And if you ignore them now, then not only was all of this for nothing but it was, in fact, all for *John Murphy*. What do you have to say about that, my friend? What do you think God has to say about that?"

Her words uncannily invoked scenes of my heated rebuke to the Muslim fanatic, Sayeet, at the Christian café, just months prior. "The most important thing," I shouted at him, "is not doing what God wants! The most important thing is doing what I want because this is . . . my program!" While I never consciously meant what I said to Sayeet, LaVerne's objectivity cut through me like a knife, forcing me to finally admit that there was more truth to that than I could have ever imagined. It shook me a bit to think that my selfishness had taken full control. The jolt that put me back on my heels, though, didn't quite knock me over just yet.

"LaVerne," I rejoined, "I understand what you're trying to say, but you have to try and put yourself in my shoes. I've been through a lot during the past two years. Not everyone would have stuck it out this long, maintaining a fairly decent attitude in spite of everything. I realize that we haven't seen any real results! That's the point! That's exactly why I'm leaving! It's pretty clear to me, by now, that producing fruit here is just not meant to be. So, as Jesus instructed His disciples, I'm just shaking the dust off my sandals and moving on. I think after a betrayal, a suicide, and some death threats, it is plain that God was speaking more loudly through all of that than He was through the tiny little events that I interpreted as 'miracles.' Does that make sense? Furthermore, I'm only planning to marry an

American. So it's about time to go home and start searching before the wrinkles start appearing and my red hair becomes a thing of the past."

"Yeah, John," LaVerne chuckled, "what makes sense to me is that YOU NEED TO REPENT, BOY!"

"Oh, really?" I sarcastically sneered.

"Yes, really!" she playfully prodded. "And the reason is because you're running from God. The saddest part of all is that you're running from Him at a time when you need Him most, but you're too blind to see it."

"How do you figure that, LaVerne?" I blurted. "What's that supposed to mean?"

"John," she explained, "God has you exactly where He wants you. At last, you've arrived at rock bottom, which, I predict, is ironically one of the greatest spiritual crests of your life. God is graciously offering you a sumptuous opportunity to spring to the next spiritual level and all you need to do is take advantage of it. Instead, you're hightailing it out of here and I'm sure that He's never been more disappointed. I know that I am!"

"Alright, LaVerne," I interrupted, "I really do appreciate your concern, but I don't think you've been able to completely grasp my situation as it really is. So, let me take this opportunity to enlighten you a little. The reason you don't have any idea what you're talking about is because you've never even been to the Muslim villages with me at all. Not once! Therefore, you can't feasibly understand how impossible my work is, and has been all along. Let me assure you, LaVerne, from my experience, that there is no potential for any kind of meaningful results in this ministry, whether in the present or even the distant future. Believe me, it's not because I haven't poured my blood, sweat, and tears into it all! Whether you've noticed it or not, that's been happening every day for the past two years. Personally, I feel that I've done all I can possibly do. What can I say, LaVerne? I gave it my best shot! I mean, that's pretty much all anyone can ever do, right? Sure, there are no happy endings here and that's just something I've learned to accept. What I refuse to accept, though, is wasting any more of my valuable time here."

Before concluding my diatribe and setting LaVerne straight for trying to set me straight, I informed her that I was nonetheless grateful for her advice. I just wasn't grateful enough to follow it.

"Wait just a second here!" she demanded. "You might have a couple of years' worth of experience in the Muslim villages on me, but I have many more years' worth of experience in the Christian walk on you! And I'm telling you, young man, that God wants to use this whole situation to stretch your faith, help you to grow leaps and bounds, and bless your life like never before. I'm not about to let you walk away from this chance without a fight because I'm 100% positive that you'll regret it for the rest of your miserable life!"

"Alright, okay," I reluctantly sighed, after a considerably long pause. "What else do you want to say to me at this point?"

"Well, John, it's like this," she explained, "I'm hereby issuing you a challenge."

"Ah, just what exactly are you getting at?" I snapped.

"Well," she replied. "I know that you've chosen the end of February as your time of departure, but I want you to know that I am so sure that God is involved in all of this that I'm willing to promise you meaningful results in your ministry if you decide to extend your stay. Even if it's just a matter of a few months, *I know* that God will come through for you on this and bless your life tremendously! That's *my promise* to you, my friend! And, rest assured, that I'll be praying along the way too! Well, what do you say to that?"

I don't know what I was thinking when I agreed. I guess I've always been a sucker for challenges and she evidently read me like a book. I have to confess that part of the reason why I invited the challenge was simply to prove her wrong, but, admittedly, I would also say that her confidence level intrigued me.

"Alright, you have yourself a deal," I grumbled. "I don't know why I'm doing this, but I'll extend my stay until the end of June, which means both you and God have four extra months to make a believer out of me. I wish you both good luck, LaVerne, but I'm not holding my breath!"

I almost didn't know where to begin ministering again since my mind was already set on leaving. My think-motor was stuck in departure gear. Simply tying up loose ends had been my main objective but now it was time to switch back into ministry gear. After all those hardcore debates with the fanatics, our cultural program and stamina were all but spent. Reviving it again didn't seem like the greatest option since most of our team, not to say anything about the Tatars themselves, had absolutely no interest in continuing with it. Nevertheless, we still gave it a lousy attempt anyway.

Two gentlemen, Husen and Igor, who had attended our program even in the midst of the ferocious squabbles, still showed some interest by sporadically popping up here and there. Now, I had been developing very casual relationships with the both of them, granted, but I didn't notice any clear indications that our friendships shared any meaningful commonality other than that of just enjoying each other's company from time to time. I was up to speed on Husen's personal quest for the truth. I knew he was privately studying both the Qur'an and the Bible, but that's all I knew until he cornered me at the Christian café, following my spiritual spat with LaVerne.

"John," he quietly confessed, "I've been doing a lot of observing lately, but have obviously chosen to keep my feelings a secret until I was sure about my intentions. I want you to know that I've been studying both books, hearing the arguments from both sides at the café, and doing some introspection regarding my personal needs. I've recently concluded that a personal relationship with Jesus Christ is what I really need most of all!"

I was floored speechless because I almost felt like Jesus, through Husen, was speaking these words to me: *"You of little faith... why did you doubt?" (Matthew 14:31)*. In any case, though my curiosity level was heightened, I still realized that there was a big difference between Husen's confidential statement to me and his public acceptance of Christ as Lord and Savior. And my uncertainty proved halfway justified.

"Oh, I'll claim to believe in Jesus and even go so far as to repent," he assured me, "but that getting-dunked-underwater-thingy just isn't doable for me because I have this mighty hunch that, if I go that far, my mother will instantly disown me. I love Jesus and all, but I love having a roof over my head too!"

Husen's good news turned out to be no news just as I had predicted. Repentance with a disclaimer attached to it definitely isn't what Jesus had in mind when He delivered His *"Good News."* Husen's definition still needed some work. In fact, his definition sounded more like partial obedience. The truth is that if you're not willing to risk everything for His sake then you're not ready to become His disciple. Husen's primary fear was the reaction of his mother, Shefikah, but let's not forget Jesus' words here: *"A man's enemies will be the members of his own household. Anyone who loves his father or mother more than me is not worthy of me... and anyone who does not take his cross and follow me is not worthy of me " (Matthew 10:36-38).*

Jesus obviously practiced what He preached by literally going to the cross for us all. During His ministry He also proved that His devotion to His Heavenly Father's will took precedent over and above Mary's wishes. Just two chapters later, in Matthew 12, Jesus demonstrates this. Christ and His disciples had been so busy ministering and healing that even their diets were somewhat affected *(Mark 3:20)*. After the news reached Mary and her sons, Mark records their reaction: *"They went to take charge of Him, for they said, 'He is out of his mind'" (Mark 3:21).* This was probably also an attempt to save Jesus from the Pharisees because His preaching was becoming fiercely pointed, due to the Jewish leaders' hateful accusations and blasphemy of the Holy Spirit *(Matthew 12:31-32)*. The logical conclusion here would further suggest that Jesus' immediate family was undoubtedly receiving flack because of His ministry. The fact that His own brothers, James, Joseph, Simon, and Judas *(Mathew 13:55)*, were all unbelievers at this stage, just added to their contempt of Him *(John 7:5)*. Incidentally, even within that very context, the apostle John describes how they cunningly tried to send Jesus into harm's way. So, needless to say, Jesus is well aware of His family's general attitude regarding His life, identity, and work. *"Someone told Him, 'Your mother and brothers are standing outside, wanting to speak to you.' He replied, 'Who is my mother, and who are my brothers?' Pointing to his disciples, he said, 'Here are my mother and my brothers. For whoever does the will of my Father in heaven is my brother and sister and mother'" (Matthew 12:47-50).* Christ understood the need to put God's will above everything else in our lives, and He did so enthusiastically. Husen, on the contrary, wasn't quite ready for that kind of commitment yet. And I had a feeling that he'd probably never be.

I still decided, Husen's hesitancy notwithstanding, to put forth my best effort to convince him that God would somehow resolve his dilemma even though I had no earthly idea how. "Husen," I argued, "if you really believe in Jesus then you've got to manifest some evidence here. God is happy to hear your confession of faith, but He would also like to see it, especially in light of the circumstances. I mean, if your fears outweigh your faith then you can't expect God to meet you halfway. I understand that your fears are real. BUT SO IS HE! You've got to believe that if Jesus is real then He can handle your situation. And, whether it's easy for me to say this or not, I believe He can! The ultimate question is: 'Do you?' Fortunately, God is giving you a chance to prove it beyond any shadow of a doubt. Oh, and let me add that this kind of opportunity is actually more like a privilege because God only bestows it on a select few. As crazy as it may sound, facing this dilemma with faith right now, may even turn out to be a special blessing in your life down the road."

Well, all of this plainly bordered on the satirical because I was beginning to sound a lot like LaVerne. I preached LaVerne's message to Husen: "THIS IS YOUR BIG CHANCE TO TRUST GOD FOR ONCE IN YOUR LIFE!" Although God simply wanted to see the proof in Husen's life, I was actually the one who needed that proof most of all. Ironically, I was trying to persuade someone to step out in faith and completely trust in God's faithfulness, despite the daunting circumstances, when I was all but assured that He'd long given up on me.

Husen put up wolfish resistance at first, but it didn't take too long before his heart softened. He mentioned that his mother was considering taking a trip back to Uzbekistan, where he was raised. He just wasn't sure when. He further insinuated that his newfound faith was starting to haunt him regarding his spiritual obligations.

"Perhaps we could consider stepping out in faith after she departs," Husen suggested.

"Well," I rejoined, "that sounds like a plan." The problem was that both of us were doubtful whether that trip would ever actually take place. Because his Mom had been talking about the possibility for over a year, it sounded more like a convenient excuse than anything else. In fact, I distinctly remember growing increasingly incredulous of people during that depressing time in my life. Too many people had reneged on their oaths for me to trust anyone. If I had grown suspicious of God, then just imagine how disillusioned I'd become with people. After dismissing Husen's proposal as a mere stalling tactic, those familiar feelings of isolation, abandonment, and even a sense of paranoia, slipped back into my soul, as if they'd never left. And June was already upon us.

The time had finally come for me to lick my wounds and plan my escape. I purchased a one-way plane ticket home, vowing never to return to this strange country. I had successfully triumphed over LaVerne by failing miserably in everything I'd done in Crimea. And nobody felt sorrier for me than yours truly, but that didn't nag me because I was too wrapped up in myself to care about anyone else's opinion. Nothing excited me more than the thought of abandoning everyone I had attempted to help along the way, and the fact that God was watching my sad production only added to my satisfaction. It was now my turn to smile, as I switched back into departure mode. That is, until mid-June, when Husen showed up on my doorstep with the latest news: "John, my mother finally bought her ticket to Uzbekistan! Can you believe it?"

"Seriously?" I questioned.

"Yes!" he affirmed. "It's definite! So, since she's leaving this weekend, I thought that you still might be willing to baptize me before you get out of here."

"Ah, are you sure about this?" I queried.

"Oh, hey," he replied, "I realize it's been quite a while since we discussed this, but I'm still here! Aren't I? I mean, that should say something, right?"

"Ah, yeah," I fumbled, "I guess you have a point there."

"You know, John," he continued, "I've been thinking about what you said a couple of months ago and I believe you're right. How can I expect Jesus, who willingly sacrificed His life for me, to save me when I'm not even willing to step out of my comfort zone just a little? That's just not fair to Him. He deserves more than that and

I'm ready to deliver. By the way, Igor also told me that he, too, is ready! The big question now is, 'Are you?'"

It was comical how the Lord spoke to me, the missionary, during both my conversations with Husen. All along, as God had been reaching out to Igor and Husen, He had also been reaching out to me. Literally, just days before my everlasting escape from Ukraine, *He found me at last.* In the cool June waters of the Black Sea, on the outskirts of Yalta, both Igor and Husen, two former Muslims, completely submitted their lives, their fears, and their wills, to the Lord Jesus Christ. It was truly a victorious moment that will not only forever change their lives, but also my own.

LaVerne's prophetic-like promise stunningly came true. I was clueless in terms of approaching LaVerne or knowing what to say to her, which was precisely how I felt in my relationship to God. At that moment, it was just time to go home, scratch all of my future plans, and follow LaVerne's wise counsel: "YOU NEED TO REPENT, BOY!"

Repenting was an area in which I had ample experience, so it was generally full speed ahead, especially following a God-lesson like that one. The Lord miraculously taught me that giving up on Him is never an option, no matter how bleak things may appear to be. Though Bible study in my early childhood days constantly emphasized that lesson, it never really registered until I experienced that for myself. The apostle Paul reminds us that even death itself shouldn't steal our hope in Him: *"The sting of death is sin, and the power of sin is the law. But thanks be to God! He gives us the victory through our Lord Jesus Christ. Therefore, my dear brothers, stand firm. Let nothing move you. Always give yourselves fully to the work of the Lord, because you know that your labor in the Lord is not in vain" (1 Corinthians 15:56-58).*

After God educated me and poured two new converts into my lap, I returned to Crimea and stayed another two and a half years. In all, thirteen former Muslims, each representing a string of tiny wonders, chose to become Christ's disciples through our ministry. Consequently, God is not only continuing the work He began in Crimea, within the Tatar communities, but He's also doing so in my own personal life.

LaVerne quickly became both a close friend and a spiritual mentor. I will always be grateful for the significant role she played in God's plan because, otherwise, I couldn't even begin to predict how my life would have turned out. Were it not for LaVerne, I can assuredly tell you that aside from missing all of God's bountiful blessings resulting from the spiritual maturity He nurtured within me, I probably would never have met the love of my life, my beautiful Russian wife, Iryna. On LaVerne's birthday, several years ago, I read a poem that I'd written for her, appropriately entitled: *"Thanks To You."* In fact, I've deliberately chosen to keep the words handy as a reminder of everything that God taught me through her keen insights. The words should speak for themselves:

Lessons learned and old habits burned, thanks to you.
Long talks on the phone, a true sense of how I've grown,
thanks to you.
A woman's view, revealing what I never knew, thanks to you.
New interests developed, and new insights enveloped,
thanks to you.
Hidden talents to the surface, and encouragement as the
preface, thanks to you.
Precious time spent, affording me the chance to vent,
thanks to you.
Worthy advice, given in a manner that's so nice, thanks to you.
A spiritual guide and a friend by my side, thanks to you.
May not always understand, yet willing to hear with heart and
hand, thanks to you.
Nowhere to turn, but then there's LaVerne, thanks to Him.
A life transformed, yes, gracefully performed, thanks to Him.
Your grace applied, as Your presence abides, thanks to You.
Your love surrounds, Your blessings abound, thanks to You.
One life, one gift, thanks to You.

Chapter Eighteen
One happy ending and a few happy beginnings

∽o∾

Back in Bible College, I missed the chance to take a course on Christian evidences since it wasn't a requirement then. In fact, if my memory serves me correctly, I recall having not even the least bit of interest in the subject. However, just before graduating, I spoke with Don Tingle, a professor from the seminary in which I had planned to enroll. He suggested that I pursue a degree in that particular field. He had previously ministered in the New York area and was well aware of my intentions of returning there.

"New York is full of unbelievers," he advised, "so I'd get some ammunition if I were you." I took his advice seriously because I had grown up there myself. I knew exactly what he was talking about. So, wanting to be adequately prepared for ministry in New York, I did just that. Of course, as you know, I never got to New York. But that was fine because God had His own agenda. He was preparing me for working with people in the former USSR, including Muslims, even though I had never even had so much as a conversation with a real live Muslim. In seminary, I took one of Don Tingle's classes. It was called *"Jesus and Islam."* We were taught how to effectively witness to Muslims, even using the Qur'an itself as a basis from which to work. While taking the class, I never even considered the possibility of serving abroad. That thought just never even occurred to me. In fact, since the class was an elective, I almost decided not to take it, arbitrarily changing my mind at the last minute. I'm sure that, by now, you've noticed that God certainly likes doing things at the very last moment.

Either way, that class, combined with the rest of my apologetics background, proved invaluable for the kind of outreach God was calling me to. It's sure good to know that God knows what He's doing whether we do or not. So, there's another one of those signs of God's sovereignty encompassing my life and ministry, as well as the lives and ministries of those He sent my way.

Before concluding this true *fairy tale* of mine, let me share just a few closing tidbits that spectacularly demonstrate God's intimate involvement in all of this. As far as Igor was concerned, none of us had any worries about his well-being because he was half Russian *(basically exempt from the pressure usually applied by the Muslim community)*, a resident in a Russian neighborhood, and was living with his Russian wife and son. Husen's case differed considerably. Husen has absolutely no Russian lineage whatsoever. He's half Uzbek and half Crimean Tatar, which means he's expected to be 100% Muslim. Moreover, he was living with his Muslim mother in a Muslim village.*

As far as Shefikah *(Husen's Mom)* was concerned, all of us were forced to play the waiting game because she was to remain in Uzbekistan for several weeks. As far as I was concerned, since my departure for the states was imminent, I'd miss seeing Shefikah upon her return. Meeting her again would have to wait until after my furlough, which was fine with me, all things considered. Although I was now thousands of miles from Husen, my prayers invariably went up for him. I knew he was terrified. He had already taken his public step of faith. The next step was confronting his mother with the truth. None of us knew what the future held for Husen; all we knew was that Mom would be home very soon. And, believe you me, that was more than enough to chew on. Word about his conversion would soon get out. Would Mom inform the leaders at the mosque? If so, what would they do? Would Mom disown him? Would he be ostracized by the community? Where would he live? What about the possibility of even more rueful scenes? Having received indirect death threats myself, I couldn't help but entertain those thoughts too. What about this? What about that? A bunch of panic and a miniscule amount of faith can really stress us out sometimes. Why couldn't we maintain our perspective? That was the real question. I mean, God had just stepped into our situation with a Grammies-styled red-carpet entrance shouting, *"Hey, ah, don't forget about Me now!"* That was undeniable. What we weren't counting on, adding to that, was the fact that God would be taking home all of the Grammies that night.

When I returned to Ukraine, I was so relieved to find out that Husen was still living at home and in very good spirits. But when I heard why that was the case, I almost fell out of my chair! Shefikah had gone to Uzbekistan for a couple of reasons, one of which was to visit her grandson. He had been hospitalized in his hometown of Termez, near the Afghan border. For Shefikah, having been raised in the city of Samarkand, Uzbekistan, Termez turned out to be an unfamiliar place entirely. On the other hand, though, it normally doesn't take whopping effort to get around in the former USSR because of the system of public transport. If you know both your bus number and the name of your bus stop, then you'll usually get to wherever you're headed.

On one particular evening, Shefikah had the chance to spend some quality time with her grandson since she was the only visitor there. Upon leaving the hospital, however, she quickly realized that she'd lost track of the time. A passing glance at her watch, while standing on the bus stop, startled her because it was after eleven o'clock in the evening. That meant she had just missed the last bus home. Lacking money for a taxi and unable to phone her daughter, it didn't take a rocket scientist to figure out that she had stumbled into a frightening little pickle. Withal, it soon became evident that this tiny quagmire would change her life forever! You see, *it was then*, which also happened to be around the same time that Husen was planning to be baptized in the Black Sea, that this seventy-year old Muslim woman claims to have had an encounter with the Son of God Himself.

According to Shefikah, having already consigned herself to the task of finding her own way home on foot, she successfully got oriented enough to initially head in the right direction, before coming to a complete standstill. In the dark, already past midnight, she reached a fork in the road that veered off in three different directions. Unable to decide which path to take, Shefikah then opted for her only remaining last resort. All she could think of doing, at that moment, was kneeling down to ask Allah for guidance. After receiving no apparent response, she began praying to Muhammad, yet again receiving nothing but a feeling of empty silence. Finally, in tears and desperation, she caustically cried out to Jesus, the one about whom her son's missionary friend had often spoken. Immediately, she felt a hand gently lift her forearm until she was on her feet. To this very day, Shefikah freely testifies that it was that invisible hand which supposedly rested on her shoulder and gently nudged her along, guiding her all the way to her daughter's doorstep. She even claims to have heard footsteps behind her, the whole way home, though she vows not to have seen anyone near her. And, before she knew it, she was standing in front of her daughter's house. "I distinctly recall," she explains, "several moments when I felt the urge to walk in one specific direction, but that gentle hand just wouldn't let me." Even now, years later, Shefikah remains fully convinced that it was the hand of Jesus Christ that delivered her that night. Moreover, she continues to boldly testify about it to anyone willing to listen.

Following Shefikah's return to the Crimean Peninsula, after Husen shared the news about his recent conversion to Christianity, you could just have imagined his astonishment upon getting her response. Rather than being maligned and evicted, Husen was the recipient of a giant hug from Mom, once the truth came out. *"The God of all comfort" (2 Corinthians 1:3)* is also the God of a million surprises. The story of Husen and Shefikah is truly an inspiring one because it reminds us of how close God really is to all of us, while showing how much He cares about our unique situations. *"Cast all your anxiety on Him because He cares for you" (1 Peter 5:7).* That's just what Husen did. He trusted the Lord to take care of him and dispel his fears, and Jesus even decided to answer that prayer in person.

In actuality, this type of instance doesn't appear to be very uncommon at all. The statistics supposedly indicate that a large percentage of Muslims who commit the second most heinous sin in Islam by accepting Jesus Christ, claim that it was originally because of some miraculous encounter with Him or a life-changing dream of some sort, convicting them against their own wills. The September 2002 issue of *Christianity Today* reports on an Afghan believer who was allegedly imprisoned by the Taliban during that summer, based upon his close connections with the Christian missionaries there. For two solid weeks he was beaten with a steel cable, at least once a day, losing consciousness completely during the final beating. That evening, he dreamt of a luminous man in white garb who kindly instructed him to get up, leading him out of his cell. On approaching the front gate, he met another man wearing bright green clothing. *(In Islam, the color green denotes God's blessings.)* It was this man who led him out of the prison. According to his testimony, this Afghan believer awoke from his dream that night only to find his cell door ajar, with no visible guards in the immediate vicinity, allowing him to walk straight out into the hallway and all the way out the front gate. Indeed, it sounds like something straight out of the pages of the New Testament. And if you happen to be skeptical about the credibility of this particular testimony, or that of Shefikah's, for that matter, then there are still hundreds of others out there for your consideration.

"Okay, well how is Husen doing these days?" you might ask. Well, I was just getting to that one. Do you remember when I told Husen that his decision to face his fears, for the cause of Christ, rather than retreating, could bring forth abundant blessings into his life? No? Well, I did. Just trust me on this one. And, as LaVerne's words became a reality, so did mine. In 1999, local doctors were understandably concerned about Husen's benign brain tumor, which had successfully dissolved a large portion of his skull. It was growing at such a rate that area physicians were worried it would eventually suffocate him, because it was rapidly expanding into his throat area. They were even speculating that he only had about five or six years to live. The tumor was a result of a hereditary skin disease, although Husen's condition seemed far worse than that of any of his close relatives. In the early eighties, Husen's burden, causing his ear to drape all the way down to the side of his neck, became so overwhelming for him that he chose to make it a matter of prayer. In one sense, for Husen, believing in God was difficult. If having been fed a daily diet of atheism from early childhood wasn't enough then we can add to that the only real perception of deity that he was ever really exposed to, which was the god of Islam. Due to the fatalistic aspects of Islam, most Muslims automatically saw Husen's physical appearance as an outward sign of Allah's curse. Life was hard. Grace was hard to come by. Consequently, retaining any authentic faith in God was an uphill battle for Husen. Thankfully, though, that was all Husen had left. "If there really is a god out there somewhere," he cried, "and you can hear me, then please help me!"

The scorn of the Muslim community squelched any desire for them to assist him in any positive way. Furthermore, Russian doctors were unwilling to tackle an operation of that magnitude because of all the risks involved. Almost immediately after Husen's conversion, however, the Christian community stepped up to bat and became an answer to his prayers. One Louisville couple, Charles and Penny Faust, after hearing about Husen's amazing story, instantly entered the picture through daily intercession on his behalf. Before long, they were also on the phone with their minister, Bob Russell, picking his brain about what might be done to help our new brother in Christ. Since Bob Russell was well known in their community, as the minister of Southeast Christian Church, one of the largest churches in North America, he was an important piece in God's puzzle. Bob's arduous demands and toilsome schedule still couldn't deter him from jumping on the bandwagon, once he heard about Husen's amazing testimony. And, incredibly, with the help of some other Christians living in Seattle, Washington, they were also able to pin-point a top-notch surgeon who willingly accepted the challenge. In fact, Dr. Joseph Gruss, from Harborview Medical Center, not only agreed to operate, but also decided to donate all of his services free of charge. Moreover, God provided a highly regarded neurologist who also joined the medical team at no cost. Nonetheless, the estimated price tag for Husen's additional needs exceeded $100,000. Needless to say, that would take quite a few prayers to collect. With all of the other pieces in the puzzle falling into place so perfectly, though, our hopes were still way up. And, let's just say that GOD DID NOT DISAPPOINT!

It's no secret that we were all a little anxious about the operation, but God gradually calmed our spirits in a variety of fascinating ways, as the time drew near. Before the surgery, I remember driving Husen from the east coast to Louisville. We were scheduled to meet with the people through whom God was working. On the way, we spontaneously decided to stop at Kentucky Christian College, in Grayson, to chat with some of our Ukrainian friends who happened to be studying there at the time. Husen was hoping that they'd pray for him. His nervous tension was almost approaching panic levels in the car, which is one of the reasons we chose to stop. He just needed some support and encouragement. Interestingly enough, although we all prayed for Husen together, the students weren't in much of a condition to console him because they were all so preoccupied with their own dreary plights. Living in a tiny Kentucky town was quite the transition for them, as was studying in an American college. They were clearly overwhelmed with their work load, the new environment, and their inability to do much about it. After getting back in the car and continuing on our way, Husen told me that he felt a lot better.

"How's that?" I asked. "Nobody really seemed to sympathize with you at all!"

"Well," he replied, "that gave me the perfect opportunity to comfort them instead. And, for some reason, I almost forgot all about my problems in the process. Now, to be quite honest, I'm really not that worried anymore."

Right after that comment, I explicitly remember sluggishly drudging our way up another one of those irksome hills, along I-64 West. Finally hitting the top, we both beheld the most gorgeous sunset I think I've ever seen in my life. There was a monstrous cloud, almost resembling a tornado spout, glistening with brilliant slithers of sunlight. The sight was so magnificent that I was sure that God had specifically painted it for us, especially since it immediately brought to mind the Old Testament image of the cloud in which God dwelt during the wilderness wanderings, after the Exodus. At that moment, I also felt much better because it seemed as though God was literally going before us, leading the way directly into His perfect plan for our friend, Husen. That picture impacted me so forcefully that I turned to Husen right away, conveying those same thoughts to him. Well, not only did Husen share similar thoughts, but we in-turn went on to share them with what seemed like half of Louisville.

Husen's story had already made the local news, in Louisville. As a result, there was one special nine-year old girl who affectionately chose to make a concerted effort to help. She was attending a private Christian school and her name was Madison. Single-handedly, Madison introduced Husen's story to all of the kids in her class, even inspiring them to band together in support of him. As you could imagine, we were also taken aback, upon visiting her class, to be met by journalists and news correspondents from the local newspapers and TV stations, waving their cameras and microphones. It was almost staggering to see how one girl's compassion could reach so many people and lend so much encouragement to all of us, when we needed it most. Although her small class only raised about $200 toward Husen's expenses, the impact God made through all of them will never be forgotten. Husen chatted with the kids and cameras as I translated for him. They were all very curious indeed. In fact, they even threw in a few presents for Husen before we left.

Topping all of that off was the very last question, posed by one of the boys in the class, just before Husen was to walk out the door: "Husen, when is your birthday?"

After answering, Madison, who had actually been very shy throughout much of the visit, sprang to her feet with the biggest smile you ever saw and shouted, "Hey, that's my birthday too!" You guessed it: another pick-me-up from *"the God of all comfort."*

Coupled with the $200 raised by Madison's class was over $100,000 raised by the Christian community. So it wouldn't be long before a date was set for Husen's big day. Usually, before a routine operation, approximately ten or twelve veins are cauterized to decrease the amount of blood flow during surgery. In Husen's case, by contrast, several hundred veins were cauterized. Yet, he still required over sixty units of blood during the operation. Dr.

Gruss labeled it the bloodiest operation he had ever performed in his thirty-year practice. Husen's entire blood supply was replenished three times within nine hours, actually matching the amount of times his heart quit beating during the surgery. Dr. Gruss, himself, noted that it was nothing shy of a miracle that saved Husen's life that day. Our favorite surgeon's claim is a stark reminder that Husen lay not only on Dr. Gruss' operating table, that day, but also on God's. Moreover, we were all subsequently informed that the local mosque, near Husen's house, had continually been praying that he would die on that operating table. Hence, there was an eerie bit of spiritual warfare in all of this too. Thankfully, God's will for Husen prevailed! The operation, while messy and scary, turned out to be a smashing success. Not only did Husen get a great new look, but he also got a second chance at life, all because he trusted Jesus Christ when the going got tough. He trusted Him in the waters of the Black Sea, and continued doing so when he admitted himself into that Seattle hospital. Why? Because the Great Physician had been operating on Husen long before Dr. Gruss ever saw an x-ray.

In one fell swoop, God wound up saving Husen's soul, his life, and my ministry. Sadly, I'm ashamed to admit, I almost forfeited it all because I was stuck in a very selfish place, which just happens to be a pretty popular place for Christians at times. Let me explain. The Church, for far too long, has focused on trying to cure the world's sin condition without first tending to its own heart condition. Only a miracle or two kept me in the ministry because I had an unhealthy obsession with getting RESULTS, preventing me from genuinely loving people without any strings attached. I had completely forgotten about the first order of business. It is so much easier to preach than it is to love, especially when we're overly fixated with results. It's easy to fall into that ulterior motives' trap because it's a very selfish place to be. The irony is that *true love*, the kind that expects nothing in return, is the real key to seeing tangible results within our own lives and in others' too. It's also the best Church Growth strategy because real love, more than anything else, invites God into the picture. So, if you really want banner results in your ministry, then concentrate on loving more effectively and authentically. Jesus said, "*A new command I give you: Love one another. As I have loved you, so you must love one another. All men will know that you are my disciples if you love one another"* (John 13:34-35).

As cheesy as it may sound to some, the truth is that what the world really does need is love, because it's love that's the key to my heart, to your heart, to the world's heart, and most importantly, to God's heart. Since Jesus preached love, lived love, and died in the name of love, I should have gotten the message from the very start. *(There's that slow learner trait rearing it's ugly head again.)* The sad reality is that if we're all too riveted with getting results, instead of with the need to love people unselfishly, as Jesus calls us to, then throwing in the towel when the fruit doesn't taste so sweet becomes irresistibly appealing. Perhaps, faulty statistics aside, that's one reason why the average American ministry fails to last more than just a couple of years or so. But if we're really serious about finding the center of God's perfect will for our lives then we need to get to where the very contented apostle Paul was, by letting the love of Christ compel us to minister *(i.e. serve)*, instead of relying on that all too common drive for success, which just about did me in.

Listen to Paul's words, in one of my favorite New Testament passages: *"For Christ's love compels us, because we are convinced that one died for all, and therefore all died. And He died for all, that those who live should no longer live for themselves but for Him who died for them and was raised again"* (2 Corinthians 5:14-15). In the end, it's Christ's LOVE that draws us to the foot of the cross, not His wisdom or even His miracles. Paul, arguably the greatest Christian minister in history, didn't care much about outward results *(see 1 Corinthians 1:16)*, allowing him to serve with pleasure regardless of how difficult things got. He was ultimately satisfied with his ministry because it was true love that was driving his heart. Similarly, when you and I can reach that particular point in our spiritual lives, nothing will be able to shake us from His mission.

*It's common knowledge that Muslims who convert to Christianity often pay with their very lives.

Concluding Remarks

⋙o⋘

Well, you made it! Before I leave you, I guess you'll vouch for me when I say that, in Ukraine, I've suffered so much that only the Russian language can adequately describe it. A few quick examples should suffice: major language blunders, being screamed at in a variety of languages, screaming at others in a variety of languages, getting arrested and unjustly detained, being followed by the KGB, having my phones tapped and my emails screened, being discriminated against because of my nationality, and receiving death threats because of my ministry. In simple English, it's just been one big blessing after another because I can confidently *(but not proudly)* say that I'm not as dumb as I used to be. God even taught me how to identify with James and Paul when they spoke of being thankful for trials, for through them I came to understand, experience, and literally believe that God's activity in our lives is REALLY REAL. I also came to realize that Paul's sermon in Athens wasn't just a bunch of words we theoretically call "Scripture," but that those words are demonstrably true and super relevant for anyone and everyone: *"From one man He [God] made every nation of men, that they should inhabit the whole earth; and He determined the times set for them and the exact places where they should live. God did this so that men would seek Him and perhaps reach out for*

Him and find Him, though He is not far from each one of us" (Acts 17:26-27).

Several years ago, a company working on the docks in Odessa, Ukraine, found a metal chest of some sort. They decided to use it for a while, even though it was filthy. Finally, one of the supervisors told a worker to clean it off, and only then did they realize that the chest was actually made of gold. In like fashion, if we allow God to clean our hearts off some, while opening our eyes and ears, even if it's just a little bit more than usual, then maybe we'll be afforded the chance to find the real desires of our hearts. That, my friend, by far, is the greatest treasure available to us. In the last few years I've come to appreciate that truth more than ever. And that will forever be my fervent prayer for you.

Believe it or not, your life enjoys the same potential as mine, for having His imminently active presence flowing in it, through it, and around it, every single day. *"For the eyes of the Lord range throughout the earth to strengthen those whose hearts are fully committed to Him" (2 Chronicles 16:9).* Now, all we have to do is keep our eyes, our ears, and our hearts wide open, as we buckle our seatbelts and head off in His direction. May God's richest blessings be yours as you continue your journey!

References

Blackaby, H., & Blackaby, R., (2001). *Spiritual Leadership*. Nashville: Broadman and Holman.

Brownell, G. (Autumn 2003 No.1). <u>Abroad: The Cosmopolite Magazine</u>. Copenhagen: VDN A/S.

Colson, C. (1985). *Who Speaks for God?* Wheaton: Tyndale.

Colson, C.W., & Santilli, V.E., (1987). *Kingdoms in Conflict*. New York: W. Morrow.

Dobson, J. (1993). *When God Doesn't Make Sense*. Wheaton: Tyndale.

eBible Deluxe Edition CD-ROM (2002). Nashville: Thomas Nelson.

Ferguson, D. (1998). *The Great Commandment Principle*. Wheaton: Tyndale.

Frangipane, F. (1989). *The Three Battlegrounds*. Cedar Rapids: Arrow.

Lewis, R., & Wilkins, R., (2001). *The Church of Irresistible Influence.* Grand Rapids: Zondervan.

Ortberg, J. (1997). *The Life You've Always Wanted: Spiritual Disciplines for Ordinary People.* Grand Rapids: Zondervan.